Not a Toff

The Life Story of
Donald Curry
Baron of Kirkharle

Jim Cockburn

malcolm down
PUBLISHING

First published 2025 by Malcolm Down Publishing Ltd
www.malcolmdown.co.uk

29 28 27 26 25   7 6 5 4 3 2 1

British Library Cataloguing in Publication Data
A catalogue record for this book is available from the British Library.

ISBN 978-1-917455-40-4

Cover design by Esther Kotecha
Art direction by Sarah Grace

Printed in the UK

Contents

Part Four: Serving the Lord in the Lords

Foreword

When Jim Cockburn and I initially discussed the writing of a book, neither he nor I fully appreciated the scale of the undertaking. Jim has spent months and months researching, interviewing and drafting for which I am enormously grateful to both him and his wife Ella, for the intrusion and disruption this must have caused in the Cockburn household.

The picture painted conveys what has been a fascinating journey of a boy growing up on a farm in rural Northumberland in a strongly Christian family, leaving school at fifteen, and then ultimately arriving in the House of Lords in 2011 as a Crossbench Peer.

The portrayal is, of course, far too generous and describes the person I aspire to be rather than the person I recognise. As the apostle Paul said in Romans 7:18 *'For I have the desire to do what is good, but I cannot carry it out.'*

Not only am I greatly indebted to Jim but also to my wife, Rhoda, whose love, patience, constant support, guidance and common sense has been so essential, and to my family for being so tolerant.

I have gathered hundreds and hundreds of friends on the way who have enriched my life, and some of whom have contributed to the content of this book. Thank you all very much indeed.

Donald Curry
July 2025

Introduction

A long-running legal investigation finally came to Exeter Crown Court in February 2019, involving allegations of corporate manslaughter against Clinton Devon Estates after a young man had been tragically killed on the estate. Andrew Landon QC led the defence of Clinton Devon Estates, and on the sixth day of the trial he called Lord Donald Curry to the stand as an expert witness. Lord Curry was chosen because he was a trustee of the estate with practical experience of working on a farm, and so knew what he was talking about. In introducing Lord Curry, Landon gave an outline of his career and ended by stating, *'I hope that he would not mind me saying that he is no "toff". He is a hill farmer and a very successful one. A man who has flourished.'* The charges against the estate were dismissed, partly as a result of Lord Curry's powerful and knowledgeable testimony. As John Varley, Chief Executive of the estate said later, *'The Crown Prosecution Service and the police just didn't realise who they were taking on.'* It had taken five difficult years of investigations to come to the conclusion that the death of the young man was indeed an accident.

The barrister claimed that Donald Curry was not a 'toff', and those who know him will agree that he is certainly not a 'toff'. There are, however, many reasons why you might think that he is. He is a member of the House of Lords, where his title is Baron Curry of Kirkharle Kt CBE. Throughout his career he has mixed with very important people, including prime ministers, Cabinet ministers, and high-ranking civil servants and public officials. He also knows His Majesty King Charles III quite well, having worked with him for about twenty-five years, meeting him every few months at either Clarence House or Highgrove, as well as on some regional visits as a result of his keen interest in rural issues and his deep concern about farming and the future of farming families. Indeed, on one occasion, when the Prince (as he then was) met Donald on the steps of Clarence House, not having seen him for about six months, he greeted him, saying, *'Hello Don. I haven't seen you for ages. I thought you must be dead!'*

Despite working with very important people, being involved in chairing important government commissions and producing highly valued reports, he has never forgotten his Northumberland farming roots. As was stated in the court case, he is at heart a practical farmer who knows the day-to-day intricacies of running a modern farming business. At the height of the BSE crisis in the 1990s he would spend whole days going from one television studio to another, being interviewed about the crisis facing agriculture. As he did so, he thought back to his days as a young Northumbrian farmer, and how that life seemed so different from what he was currently doing. Farming was in his blood, however, and he wanted to do all that he could to help struggling farmers who were facing the loss of their livestock.

He has never forgotten the love he had for growing up on a farm in the beautiful Coquet Valley in Northumberland, or when he obtained his first farm tenancy at Kirkharle. He has never forgotten the dedicated, hardworking people that he laboured alongside in his early farming days; many of them he still sees when he is back home in Northumberland. The Northumberland countryside where he and his wife Rhoda raised their family remains a source of joy to him, a place where they mixed with friends and family in close farming communities. Sadly, he and Rhoda, like so many other couples, faced family tragedies, which brought them closer to those in similar situations.

Perhaps more than anything, what stands out about Donald is the personal humility he displays when he reflects on his work and relates it to others. As he put it himself, *'Every time I walk into the House of Lords, and look around at the walls, I ask myself, "Why am I here?" It's amazing.'* He knows, given his humble origins and his own self-awareness, that he was an unlikely recipient of a peerage and the title of Baron Curry – unless, of course, it was part of some greater plan, which is what Donald actually believes. He knows that it was very much by God's grace that he has been given all the important positions that he has held in his life – positions that he did not necessarily deserve but were bestowed upon him by the grace of God.

Donald's Christian faith is central to his life. His humility is a reflection of the humility of Christ, who *'being found in appearance as a man, he humbled himself by becoming obedient to death – even death on a cross!'*[1] He sees the great example of Jesus, and wants to display that same humility in all of the situations in which he finds himself. He desires to follow the command of Paul when he says, *'Do nothing out of selfish ambition or vain conceit. Rather, in humility value others above yourselves, not looking to your own interests but each of you to the interests of others.'*[2] That is the standard he tries to maintain in his life.

Rev. Dr Gordon Gatward, one of his friends who has worked alongside him over a number of years in a range of agricultural roles, very powerfully summed up Donald's character as follows:

> *He is the most humble of men. He has tremendous compassion – he genuinely cares for others. He has a Christ-like character. I have never heard him get ratty, even in difficult meetings. He was a good person to turn to in adversity.*

Let us explore the life of this amazing man, and we shall indeed discover that he is not a 'toff'.

---

1. Philippians 2:8
2. Philippians 2:3-4

PART ONE

Family, Farming and Faith

CHAPTER ONE

Family Life:
From Childhood to Wedding Day

The Currys and the Murrays

The Currys and the Murrays were well-known farming families in the border counties, and had intermarried for generations. Both families were very prolific (to use an agricultural term) and had helped populate these counties. Therefore, when Robert Thomas Younger Curry (known as Rob) married Barbara Ramsay Murray, it would be regarded by both families as a very suitable match.

As was customary amongst farming families in those days, Barbara moved into the family home on the farm at Low Burradon, with Granny, Rob's mother, very much in charge. This must have been a difficult experience for a young bride living and working within her mother-in-law's domain. It was hard for Rob as well, as Granny took many of the main farming decisions. For example, when the Harbottle Estate put the farm up for sale in 1957 for £7,500, Rob wanted to buy it, but Granny was unenthusiastic and put her foot down, saying, '*It will be a millstone around our necks for the rest of our lives.*'

Donald was born to Rob and Barbara on 4th April 1944 (4.4.44!), which was a very inconvenient time to have a baby as it was at the height of the lambing season. This meant that Barbara would be out of action on the farm at the most demanding time of the year. Donald weighed six pounds seven ounces when he was born. Robbie Brodie, the son of a shepherd and who worked for Rob, and who had witnessed numerous attempts to revive weakly lambs, was not very sure about Donald's prospects. He said rather dismissively, '*Yu might rear him, but a hev ma douts.*'

Despite Robbie's misgivings, Donald grew and developed well. Rob and Barbara kept up their families' reputation of being prolific and had more children: Joyce, Sheena, Stuart and finally, in 1961, Christopher. Donald was seventeen when Chris was born, and was quite embarrassed at the birth of his new baby brother. As he himself put it, '*Reproduction is what happens on a livestock farm, but I couldn't believe that my parents were "still doing it" at their age.*' By the age of seventeen Donald was a gangly youth and at least seven inches taller than his father. He felt particular embarrassment when his father met people and told them that Donald was his son and '*I have them from six foot four to eighteen inches.*'

Life on the Farm

Donald's childhood days at Low Burradon were ones of great happiness for him, enjoying fun in the fresh air, amongst the animals and the machinery, carrying out the farmyard tasks allocated to him. Post-war farms had mixed farming systems, and each farm had a large variety of animals and crops, unlike the specialist farms that we have today.

This was the period of post-war austerity with ration books and coupons. Like so many post-war rural families, the Curry family was not particularly well off, but they did not suffer undue privations. There was little evidence of obesity amongst the population, and nor was there any waste. Barbara could produce a meal from next to nothing. Joints of meat were cooked on a Monday, served cold on a Tuesday, chopped up and mixed with mashed potatoes and turnip then fried up for Wednesday and possibly Thursday. The bones were boiled to make soup. Any household waste was fed to the hens or the pigs. Unused bread was turned into bread-and-butter pudding. Rabbits and pigeons were shot and made into pies. A pig was killed every year and fed the family throughout the following year. If friends arrived unexpectedly, Barbara was always able to find something in the pantry to provide a very satisfying meal. The family enjoyed a simple lifestyle with enough to meet their needs, with a bit extra left over to provide hospitality to others.

There were of course foodstuffs and other supplies that came from beyond the farm. Home deliveries were commonplace in the 1950s, although it would of course be many decades before orders were placed using computer technology. A bread van arrived on the farm twice a week and George Dodds, the butcher, came every Thursday, delivering orders and bringing the gift of a sausage for each child. As George said, '*It encouraged them to be meat eaters.'* Willie Rutledge delivered the grocery order from Rothbury. A van also brought a large stock of hardware, supplying anything that might be needed in the kitchen. It also carried an oil tank on the back to replenish the farm's supply of paraffin.

Paraffin was necessary because, as Donald recalls, they did not have electricity until he was ten years old. One of his tasks when he returned from school each evening was to fill all the lamps with paraffin oil and replace any candles as required in the candlesticks. This was an important responsibility, as these lamps were necessary if any outside work had to be done. They were also necessary for Donald's evening activities, including homework, reading, crafts and hobbies such as stamp collecting.[3]

There were jobs on the farm or in the house for everyone from a very early age. As Donald himself said, *'I and my siblings were born with little wellies on.'* The pet lambs had to be fed, calves had to have their water buckets filled up, meal had to be mixed with household food waste for the hens, eggs had to be collected and pigs had to be fed. There were two milking cows that had to be hand milked both morning and evening, and all muck from the cows, pigs and hens had to be cleaned out by hand.

As a young person growing up on the farm, Donald saw technology changing. One of his earliest memories was as a three-year-old being lifted up on the back of Bobby, a lovely Clydesdale and the last working horse on Low Burradon. *'This was a scary experience, like being on the*

---

3. Donald is still a keen philatelist, having first-day covers from 1956.

top of a moving mountain.' Fordson tractors were, however, soon to arrive on the farm, and began to replace the likes of Bobby in towing trailers and other farm machinery. Eventually the 'Old Fordson' itself was replaced by the 'Grey Fergie', which used hydraulic power and was named after the inventor and mechanic Harry Ferguson who developed it. His invention using hydraulics transformed the agricultural world, as farms of all different sizes across the country employed the 'Grey Fergie'.

Harvest time was a very busy time on the farm, and even with the use of the Massey Harris combine harvester, it was still very labour intensive. There was barely time to eat, so Barbara brought lunch out to the workers in the field in heavy baskets. After a morning's work, the labour force looked forward to their jam sandwiches and the tea that Barbara had placed in glass lemonade bottles inside woollen socks to keep it hot. Farming families are notorious for eating their food at breakneck speed. Donald's father Rob would often describe them as *'pigs at a trough; those that eat the fastest get the most'.*

Another exceptionally busy time on the farm was lambing season. Rob looked forward to it each year with great anticipation; indeed, it was almost an obsession with him. He had about two hundred and fifty ewes, all Scotch Halfbreds, and he loved all of them. Amazingly, considering that the ewes all had completely white faces and were seemingly indistinguishable, he knew them individually, often talking to them about the lambs they bore the previous year. One is reminded of Jesus as the

Good Shepherd in John's Gospel, when he said, '*I am the good shepherd; I know my sheep and my sheep know me.*'[4]

The rams (or tups as they were called in farming circles) were 'put out' among the ewes on Rob's birthday, 28th October, which meant that with a five-month gestation period, the ewes were due to 'lamb down' on 25th March. The tups had been 'keeled', which involved putting on them each day a thick coloured paste that would mark the ewes when they had been tupped. The colour was changed each week for three weeks, so that the different coloured ewes could be segregated and brought into the lambing field in order of date to 'lamb down'.

Much time was spent in preparation for the birth of new lambs. Lambing pens, which were used in adverse weather or if a ewe was in difficulty, had to be repaired. Trailer loads of swedes were scattered round the fields for the ewes to eat after they had given birth. New marker pens and iodine were purchased to treat the lambs' navels after birth. Rob also bought a couple of dozen bottles of stout in case his energy levels dropped too low from working long hours; they were hidden in a cupboard under the stairs, so that nobody would see him having a quick swig.

Rob's other great obsession was Old English Game birds, so much so that he became President of the Old English Game Club for ten years. After he died in 1979, his obituary appeared in the May 1979 edition of *Fur and Feather* magazine. There were game birds everywhere at Low Burradon, as they nested in hay sheds, barns, tractor

---

4. John 10:14

sheds and even in the machinery, covering everything with hen muck. He had different sheds and runs for different strains, such as Duckwings, Brown Reds, Piles and Greys. He was renowned for his Greys, and was considered to have the best strain of Greys in Britain; this was a great accolade in his world. He would take his birds to shows not only within the region, but also to national shows such as at Olympia in London.

Education

At the age of five Donald did not really want to go to school. Granny was the only person who showed any sympathy for Donald's feelings, saying, *'If he doesn't want to go to school, just let him stay at home.'* Her pleadings were ignored. Rob drove him to his first day at Netherton School. Donald cried when Rob dropped him off, and he continued to cry when Miss Fairbairn, the headteacher, held him up to watch his dad drive away. He thought that he had been abandoned and decided at that moment that he was not going to this awful place anymore. After five days of protest, he finally succumbed and settled down to what was to be his lot for the next few years.

He and other children from the Burradon area walked to school and back each day, looking at what the farmers were doing in the fields, inspecting birds' nests in the hedges and kicking pebbles down the road. There was a shop near the school run by old Mr Kidd, and Donald was occasionally allowed to use a rationing coupon to buy sweets. It was a delight when rationing came to an end and they were allowed to use real money (including farthings and halfpennies) to buy sweets, although some pupils from the school did on one occasion use toy money to obtain sweets from the unsuspecting Mr Kidd. He reported the deceit to the school; the culprits confessed, and were duly reprimanded.

Netherton School had about forty-five pupils, ranging in age from five to fifteen, all in the same room, taught by Miss Fairbairn and Mrs Green. The curriculum of the school was based on the three Rs – reading, writing and arithmetic – and gave them a good foundation of the basics. Unfortunately, Miss Fairbairn and Mrs Green left in the year before Donald's Eleven Plus examination, and were replaced by Mr and Mrs Burn. This was rather unsettling for the school. Whether that was the reason or not, Donald unfortunately failed his Eleven Plus, and so was not able to attend Morpeth Grammar School. Rob and Barbara were very disappointed and decided that they were not going to trust Tom Burn with Donald's academic future, so looked at other educational options.

There was a school at Haydon Bridge that looked very attractive as it had a school farm and two of Donald's cousins, John and Walter Murray, were already students there. He and his parents were invited for interview with the headmaster, Edward Waite. The big mistake that they made was not preparing for the interview; Rob and Barbara had never been interviewed in their lives, and for Donald it was a completely alien experience. When he was asked why he wanted to come to Haydon Bridge, he mumbled something about his cousins being there and they seemed to enjoy it, which was not really the answer that Mr Waite was looking for.

Needless to say, Donald's application was unsuccessful, and he himself felt rejected and unworthy. Perhaps, however, it was the jolt that he needed to push himself forward. His parents found Morpeth Commercial College, which seemed an unlikely choice, but Donald was accepted there and stayed until the age of fifteen. The college was run by Major Davies, a rather severe-looking man with a moustache who clearly enjoyed retaining his military title, as his specialty was discipline. Donald remembers him well. *'He played the piano for assembly each day, but had a limited repertoire. We seemed to sing "Holy, Holy, Holy" three times a week!'* This in fact turned out to be a wise choice of school, as the curriculum suited Donald's interests. In addition to the core curriculum that all schools had to teach, Donald studied commercial subjects; he revelled in the study of book-keeping and commerce, which he saw as being of great use in running a farm. After two years he left with a few Royal Society of Arts certificates, and as he appreciated, *'a more open mind'.*

After he left school, Rob told Donald that he had to think seriously about his future. He suggested auctioneering, but Donald felt that he could not possibly make his mouth work fast enough to be an auctioneer. Instead Donald replied to his father, *'It's too late. I only want to come home and work on the farm.'* As he later explained, *'I'd been indoctrinated from the day I was born!'*

That is indeed what he did, and he took an active role in the life of the farm, including some heavy manual work. Some of the heaviest work was associated with growing swedes for feeding the sheep. In the year after he left school, weeds were unusually widespread amongst the swedes, and their removal involved Donald creeping along each drill on hands and knees, pulling out the weeds as he went. This hard labour resulted in blisters on each finger, broken nails and lumps of swede lodged underneath the nails. Harvesting the swedes was also back-breaking: the swedes were pulled up by the leaves in the left hand, and both the roots and the leaves had to be chopped off with a turnip pic (blade) held in the right hand. In frosty weather, hands would get numb, and it would be very easy to chop the forefinger on the left hand and not be aware until the blood flowed; Donald still bears a scar as a result.

Perhaps Rob thought that these heavy tasks would put Donald off farming for good, but if anything it had the opposite effect. Donald absolutely loved the work. He did, however, continue his education by going to Kirkley Hall, the local agricultural college, on a day-release basis. The subjects that he studied at the commercial college laid the foundation for these studies at the agricultural college. He particularly enjoyed farm management and accounting, which would be of great value to him in his future career.

Although academic achievement was not a high priority in Donald's life at this time, he was eventually to see its value. He was much later in his life awarded three honorary university degrees for his services to agriculture. His son Jonathan later remarked that he thought it very unfair that he had to study for four years to be awarded a degree, whereas his father was given three degrees without a single day's study!

Faith

Donald's family belonged to the Christian Brethren, and worshipped at an assembly in Thropton, now called Armstrong Hall. The family went there three times a day on a Sunday for different services: the breaking of bread (communion), a Bible study and a gospel service. There were also fellowship meetings during the week and special meetings when a number of assemblies came together. Some might have regarded it as a rather strict upbringing, but Donald and his siblings enjoyed the security and stability of being brought up by loving Christian parents. He described it as *'a great experience, with Christian parents, Christian families, all of the friends we had were Christians, and we were part of a large family network'.*

It was important for Donald to come to a living faith himself, and not simply rely upon the faith of his parents. Evening services at the assembly tended to be gospel services, when different speakers would come week by week and preach on the necessity of repentance from sin and a personal faith in Christ. One particular Sunday evening when he was thirteen, Donald felt that God was speaking to him directly, and so he made a personal commitment to Christ.

God spoke to me that night and the message hit home, even though I had heard it week after week after week. It is amazing how at one point in time the Holy Spirit was at work, and I suddenly for the first time thought that I had to do something about it – this was for me – I need to make a personal commitment. I did, and it was absolutely a life-changing experience.

When Donald went back to school the following day, however, he did not tell others about his new-found faith; he needed further prompting from God to do that. This prompting came through a young man in the school who became a Christian at a Billy Graham meeting, and told all of his schoolmates the following day what had happened to him. For Donald, this was a rallying call from God that he needed to stand up and be counted, so that he could follow the words of Paul, *'For I am not ashamed of the gospel, because it is the power of God that brings salvation to everyone who believes.'*[5] He made a public stand at school, and although he suffered a bit of scoffing, he continued the walk with God that he had begun, albeit encountering ups and downs along the road that all young Christians face.

Part of his Christian service in his late teenage years and into his twenties involved working with others of his generation to organise youth events, which were called 'squashes' in the 1950s and '60s. These squashes were started by Ian Ross, an Edinburgh vet who spent a lot of time in ministry with young people. He understood that Christian young people wanted to come together to seek fellowship and support in Christian meetings beyond the normal church programme. Initially the young people from the Rothbury area travelled up to Edinburgh to attend the meetings, until later Ian started a meeting in the home of John and Lilian Lee in Powburn, where as many as a hundred or more young people would come together for Christian fellowship. Keith, their son, recalled these meetings in his parents' home: *'People would be sitting in*

---

5. Romans 1:16

the room, in the hall, right up the stairs. That's why they called it a "squash", because people were squashed.'

The turnout was amazing for a rural community. Young people from the Brethren assemblies enjoyed coming together for Christian fellowship in an informal setting, without the rules imposed by some of the older members of the assembly, such as the requirement for girls to wear hats. They also felt free to bring their friends. Eventually Ian passed on the leading of the squashes to Donald, Keith and Donald's cousin, John Murray.

We have already mentioned the gift of hospitality that Donald's mother Barbara had in being able to provide for unexpected visitors. Her reputation grew in the period of the squashes, as she entertained those who came to speak, along with some of the young people who came to the meetings. On weekends when squashes were taking place, it was not unusual for about a dozen teenagers to be staying at Low Burradon, and many can still recall how amazing Barbara was in welcoming people into her home and feeding them excellent meals, almost at the drop of a hat.

Over time, demand was such that these meetings outgrew homes, and so events were organised in village halls. Donald, Keith and John took responsibility for organising youth rallies at Hedgeley Village Hall, near Alnwick. Again, very large numbers of young people attended these meetings regularly. The programme had singing, testimonies, talks, and food to be shared afterwards. Many young people became Christians, as it was a safe environment in which to bring non-Christian friends to hear the message of the gospel. The squashes ran from the early 1960s to the late '80s, with succeeding generations of young Christian people taking the lead. As Donald said looking back, '*It was a real time of fellowship for young people, and there were a lot of blessings coming through this, with many coming to a faith in Christ at these events.*' These events had a major influence on Donald himself, as he felt blessed that he was able to serve in this way.

This coming together of Christian young people at different events brought someone very special into Donald's life, Rhoda Murdie. They first met at a fellowship meeting at the assembly in Alnwick on Good Friday in 1961, when Donald spotted a lovely girl with light brown, curly hair. Rhoda had also spotted Donald, and asked a mutual friend to introduce her to him. This was the first of many meetings at various youth gatherings. Donald was absolutely smitten by this lovely girl that he was getting to know; she had a lively mind, was rather rebellious and was athletic as well, having achieved as a sixteen-year-old the Northumberland County Schools record for the one hundred yards race. Eventually Donald asked her out, and they walked along Alnmouth beach. Donald remembers that occasion very well: '*I plucked up courage and took hold of her hand. It was a tender, rather innocent and very exciting moment.*'

They became engaged in 1965 and set their wedding date for 22nd September 1966. Just as Donald's entry into the world did not come at a particularly convenient time for the local farming community because it was at the height of the lambing season, their wedding date came at another very busy time in the agricultural calendar, the middle of the harvest.

The wedding took place in Alnwick Methodist Church, and about one hundred and twenty people came to the church service and the subsequent reception at the White Swan Hotel. The service was taken by Ian Ross, who had previously been such a support to them in establishing the squashes. Ian had three key words in his sermon, all beginning with 'C': *'Consider'*, *'Commit'* and *'Continue'*. These words came from Bible verses:

> For **consider** him that endured such contradiction of sinners against himself, lest ye be wearied and faint in your minds. [6]

> **Commit** thy way unto the LORD; trust also in him; and he shall bring it to pass.[7]

> But **continue** thou in the things which thou hast learned and hast been assured of, knowing of whom thou hast learned them.[8]

Ian was encouraging them in their married life together: firstly, to consider when times are difficult how much Jesus suffered; secondly, to commit their paths to the Lord; and thirdly, to continue in the way that God had taught them. To help them remember these key words, Rhoda got a local artist to do three miniature paintings of the texts; these miniatures are sitting on their piano to this day.

Donald and Rhoda have supported each other in married life for almost sixty years, holding to the words given to them on their wedding day, and have raised three children:

---

6. Hebrews 12:3 (Authorised King James Version)
7. Psalm 37:5 (Authorised King James Version)
8. 2 Timothy 3:14 (Authorised King James Version)

Jonathan, Jane and Craig. They are also a source of wisdom and encouragement for their extended family and their many friends.

CHAPTER TWO

Farming, Hospitality and Faith

A Dream Come True

After spending a blissful honeymoon in Oban and Fort William, the newly married couple settled down to life together. They rented a farmhouse for the next five years at Burradon Windyside. Donald continued to work for his father Rob on the family farm, while Rhoda transferred from working in Lloyd's bank in Alnwick to the branch in Rothbury. They relied very much on Rhoda's income, as there were times in the year when Rob could not afford to pay Donald a proper wage; it was not uncommon on family farms for sons and daughters to be given 'in kind' financial help. It was clear that there was not enough income from the family farm at Low Burradon to support all the family, and so Donald and Rhoda were unable to generate surplus capital.

This was very frustrating for Donald as he was desperate to start his own business. Donald and Rhoda did, however, seek ways to supplement their income. For example, they decided to convert some of the outbuildings at Burradon

Windyside to rear calves on a contract basis. This required them to take in week-old calves and rear them for twelve weeks; for this service they received payment from the farmers. They developed a good reputation for rearing healthy calves, as well as building up a much stronger bank balance.

Although he had his frustrations, Donald very much appreciated what Rob had done for him in teaching so many practical skills. In addition to the skills that Rob had taught him, through the courses that he had taken at Kirkley Hall he had acquired other technical skills, such as an understanding of farm accounts, an interest in farm management, and the science behind crop and animal husbandry. He now wanted to prove himself, and resolved that he would start his own business, be responsible for his own decisions, make his own mistakes, and not be obligated to other members of his family. Rhoda very much supported him in this ambition. Together he and Rhoda started to look for farm tenancies.

His Uncle Tom and Aunt Maisie (Barbara's sister) were key players in the search for a tenancy. He was close to them from his schooldays in Morpeth, when he would stay with them at Benridge Moor near Morpeth when Low Burradon was snowed in. They knew that his father did not have enough surplus capital to contribute financially to obtaining a tenancy, but because they had no children of their own and they had sold their own farm, they were prepared to give Donald and Rhoda a loan. This propelled them into action in the search for a tenancy.

They scoured the *Newcastle Journal*, the *Farmers' Weekly* and many magazines for possible opportunities, and travelled the length and breadth of the country in their search, even flying to Kent to see one farm. They had, however, no success. They tendered for some farms but were immediately rejected, or, if they were given an interview, they were disappointed when they were politely turned down. All of this caused Donald great frustration.

By 1971, when Donald was twenty-seven, they had at that stage two children: Jonathan who had been born in 1969, and Jane who was born in January of that year. There had been, however, severe complications with Jane's birth. When she was born in Rothbury Cottage Hospital, Jane had difficulty breathing, initially being starved of oxygen. In order to try to compensate for that, she ended up being given too much oxygen. The overall consequence was that she suffered brain damage, and so after birth she failed to develop as a child normally would. Her severe learning disability meant that Donald and Rhoda had to give her a lot of time and attention, and it was tough for both of them. For example, she could not feed herself or dress herself. She did not walk until she was nine, and even then, because her leg muscles had not developed properly, she required calipers on her legs.

Not being able to find a farm tenancy and now having a child with severe disabilities very much tested their faith. Yet they still believed that God would see them through their difficulties. Then, in answer to their prayers, a very desirable tenancy came up on their doorstep.

Kirkharle was a very well-known farm with a high profile when it was farmed by Fenwick Jackson. With the support of chemicals giant Imperial Chemicals Industries (ICI), he developed the eighteen-month beef finishing system where dairy-bred bull calves were reared and then sold on for beef production. Donald was an admirer, and so when its tenancy was advertised he had to go and see it. Because Jane was very young and required much attention, Rhoda could not accompany Donald, and so he took his father Rob to view the farm.

Donald was enthused by what he saw (although, as he admitted, *'I had been enthused before'*). It was a manageable size, around two hundred and eighty acres, had reasonable buildings but had a monstrosity of a farmhouse. Rob's description of this huge farmhouse to Rhoda and Barbara was very graphic: *'You could drive a Mini car down the passage, and the bed in the main bedroom looked like a stamp on an envelope!'*

Donald set about drafting a three-year farm business plan, consulted his Uncle Tom over what financial aid they could give, and after much deliberation he decided on a rent to offer. He sent off the offer and, as patiently as they could, they awaited a response. After three weeks Donald received a letter informing him that he was to be interviewed. On the day of the interview he sat in a dimly lit office in Little Harle Tower, concentrating on the questions put to him by the landowner, Major George Anderson, trying to provide intelligent answers, and hopefully presenting a better picture of his abilities than he did when interviewed by Edward Waite at Haydon Bridge High School. The key question that perhaps clinched the whole interview was when Major Anderson asked him, *'So you know Charles Foster? He and I were on the WarAg[9] together.'* The land agent who was also on the panel wanted to ask Donald questions about his financial circumstances, but Major Anderson brushed him aside. Charles Foster was one of the owners of Low Burradon, the family farm, and so clearly if the Curry family were good enough for Charles Foster, they were good enough for him. A week later Donald received a letter confirming that he had been granted the tenancy of Kirkharle.

For Rhoda this was *'a dream come true'.* They had gone through a difficult patch with the birth of Jane and bringing up their young family while trying to obtain a farm tenancy. God had made them wait, but he gave them a tenancy on their doorstep. When Donald looked back he very much saw the kindness of God providing for his family. They had only saved £1,000 of their own capital, and so they should not have been considered financially suitable for this farm, but God used the connection between Major Anderson and Charles Foster to bring about his plan for Donald's family.

Kirkharle meant so much to Donald and Rhoda that forty years later, when he entered the House of Lords, Donald asked John Anderson, Major George Anderson's grandson, if he could use Kirkharle as the title of his seat in the Lords. John Anderson very graciously agreed.

---

9. 'WarAg' was a wartime committee with the responsibility of encouraging farmers to increase their productivity and maximise their output for the war effort.

Farming Kirkharle

Now that Donald and Rhoda had obtained Kirkharle, they set about working to make it a successful business. Much of the early business was founded on rearing calves for themselves or on contract for other farmers. These were dairy-bred male calves that were reared for beef production. Over the time that they farmed Kirkharle, Donald reckons that they would have reared thousands of calves.

It was an intensive, continuous process. They had a calf-rearing shed which housed fifty-five calves, with fifty-five buckets for feeding them milk twice a day. After five or six weeks, the calves were weaned off milk and moved into another building in batches of ten or twelve, and then another fifty-five calves would come into the shed. The shed had to be completely disinfected between each batch, which in itself was hard work. On one occasion a neighbouring farmer, Hugh Robson, called and was astonished to see fifty-five buckets standing near their back door waiting to be washed. He exclaimed, '*Hey, Donald, do you have a calf for every one of them buckets?*' Donald replied that he had. To which Hugh retorted, '*I've never seen so many buckets in ma life.*'

The calves that were brought on to the farm came from across the north of England. Most were bought from Leo Robson who toured dairy farms, mostly in Cumbria, looking for calves to sell on to farms such as Kirkharle that specialised in rearing calves. When purchasing calves from a range of farms, the risk of bringing in disease, such as various strains of e-coli, salmonella and pneumonia, is high, and it can spread quickly. As a result, veterinary bills were very high.

As well as rearing calves, the farm grew cereals and there were ten acres of potatoes, which local ladies helped to harvest. Donald originally did not want to have a sheep enterprise on the farm, knowing from experience how much work was involved, particularly at lambing season. He was, however, obliged to take on sheep because without them there would have been a gaping hole in their cash flow at certain times of the year when there was no other income.

There was also scope for another type of business. The farmhouse at Kirkharle was, as we have already mentioned, a massive building, and is historically noteworthy as the birthplace of 'Capability' Brown, the famous eighteenth-century gardener and landscape architect. The northern end of the building was semi-derelict, but it was ideal for a bed-and-breakfast business. Rhoda was very keen to run such an enterprise as she was limited in what she could do on the farm, with the heavy demands on her in having to look after Jane. It would provide a helpful, indeed essential, supplement to the farm's income, and so Donald and Rhoda decided to go ahead with the renovation of the northern end of the farmhouse.

The position of the farm, just off the A696, was an ideal stopping-off point for visitors travelling north to Scotland. Three bedrooms were available, with the possibility of a fourth if necessary by using one of the children's rooms. There was only one guest bathroom, which was considered adequate as in the 1970s and '80s there was not the expectation of having an en-suite attached to each bedroom. Because it was the first farmhouse bed-and-breakfast on the A696 north of Newcastle, it attracted lots of visitors, and people of different nationalities broke their journey to stay at Kirkharle. One American group of visitors was fascinated by the cast-iron bars on the downstairs windows that had been placed there as protection against border raiders from Scotland in earlier, less-civilised times. These tourists were going to Scotland to trace their family tree, and were intrigued to think that they were staying in a house that might well have been raided by their ancestors!

The house was also used by family members. Jonathan and Craig enjoyed their holidays when their cousins came to stay at the house. For children it was a place of great adventure as together they explored the surrounding countryside. They looked back with very fond memories of the happy times at Kirkharle.

Expanding the Business

The business at Kirkharle was well established, so Donald and Rhoda looked for opportunities to expand by taking on other farms. The first one they took on was Middle Farm in Barrasford, which they farmed from 1980 to 1990 on a share-farming arrangement with Capheaton Estates. This meant that they had full access to the land but they did not have access to the farmhouse. The landlord, John Browne-Swinburne, had let the house to another tenant, and so they kept on the tenancy of Kirkharle until 1982.

In 1982 they had the opportunity to take on Frolic Farm, which was also part of Capheaton Estates, and so they relinquished the tenancy of Kirkharle and moved to their new home on Frolic Farm. They did, however, still work the farm at Kirkharle on a partnership basis with John Anderson until 1992.

The move to Frolic made business sense at the time, but Donald admits that on reflection, from a family point of view, it was probably a serious mistake, going as far as to say, 'Our time at Frolic was definitely the most difficult period of our lives.' Whereas staying at Kirkharle was a very happy time for the family, life at Frolic was more difficult. It was the time that they came to the very emotional conclusion that they could no longer care for Jane at home. They had carried out major renovations to create a bedroom and bathroom for Jane on the ground floor. By the time Jane was fourteen, however, Donald and Rhoda were finding it increasingly difficult to cope with her disabilities. They decided that they should find a residential home for her, which was one of the hardest decisions they had to make. They prayed about it a lot, as they felt that they were failing God by not being able to look after a child that he had specially given them.

It was a huge relief and answer to prayer when Jane was offered a place at Stelling Hall near Stocksfield, one of the National Children's Homes. Driving from Frolic Farm to take Jane to Stelling Hall, a mere ten miles, seemed to Donald one of the longest journeys of his life. As he remembered it, 'She seemed so vulnerable and innocent and I could not explain to her what was taking place. When I dropped her off, she stood at the door and watched me drive away. I wept all the way home and still feel very emotional when I think about it.' This was a major wrench, not just for Donald but also for the whole family, and, in particular, it coloured Rhoda's view of Frolic Farm.

Through what was certainly once more an example of God's providence, in 1990 John Browne-Swinburne offered Donald and Rhoda a lifetime tenancy of Middle Farm, which replaced the share-farming arrangement they had before. This meant that they could move into the Middle Farm farmhouse, which Rhoda loved as soon as she saw it. They stayed in the farmhouse until they retired from farming in 2018, when they moved to an apartment in Corbridge.

By the 1980s, Donald was looking for an opportunity to expand the business by taking on a hill farm to complement his lowland enterprises. His idea was to breed sheep on the hill farm as replacements for the lowland farm sheep, and have an integrated system for cattle, with a suckler cow beef herd on a hill farm, breeding calves which could be finished on the lowland farm. He already had straw that he could supply to a hill farm, and most of the farm machinery needed for silage making and other operations.

A friend called Mark Robertson had just purchased a hill farm called Soppit Farm near Elsdon. As it happened, Mark had some spare land on his farm, and gave Donald the opportunity to begin to have a suckler herd and some hill sheep. Although it was a bit far from his other operations, it provided Donald with initial experience of hill farming, until he found a more permanent arrangement nearer home.

The hill farm that he found was to be the last new farm that Donald and Rhoda farmed before they retired. That was a hill farm called Hawick Farm near Kirkwhelpington, and they farmed that from 1984 to 2001. How they obtained that was yet another example of God's providence, this time through a road traffic accident. As Donald came out of a gateway on the A696, he collided head on with a car that had come round a bend rather quickly. The driver of the other car was Lord Terence Devenport, landlord of the Rae Estate. In the ambulance on the way to hospital, they got talking about their farming interests. A year later, the tenancy of Hawick Farm came up, and Lord Devenport, no doubt remembering their conversation in the ambulance, agreed for Donald to take it on, with its large herd of suckler cattle and flock of hill sheep. They obtained a further four hundred acres when a neighbouring farm, Ferneyrigg, was split up. Eventually they had one hundred and seventy breeding cattle and about a thousand ewes on Hawick Farm.

Although Donald's farming business was very successful, it was not without difficulty. One major crisis was the foot-and-mouth outbreak of 2001. The disease was confirmed in a pig sent from a farm at Heddon-on-the-Wall in Northumberland to an abattoir in Essex. By the time it was diagnosed, the disease had spread to over a hundred farms all over the United Kingdom. The owner of the farm at Heddon-on-the Wall in Northumberland where the disease started was banned from keeping livestock for fifteen years for not informing the authorities of a 'notifiable disease'.

It was imperative to stop the disease spreading, and so an immediate slaughter of infected animals took place, including a 'contiguous cull' of animals on neighbouring land. Because they were on a contiguous farm, Donald had over two hundred cattle slaughtered. By the end of the year the disease was under control, but nationally six million cows and sheep (seven per cent of all cattle and fifteen per cent of all sheep) had been slaughtered, a devastating economic loss to the farming community nationwide, and, of course, a devastating experience for many farming families.[10]

As the business expanded it inevitably became more difficult to manage, especially when, as we shall see in later chapters, Donald was increasingly away from home dealing with matters of concern to the farming community across the nation. As he himself put it, he *was running a complicated business from the end of a telephone line in London*. Although he had good people that he could rely on, such as John Charlton and his wife Fiona who managed Middle Farm, and Rud Graham, his wife Lesley and their son Ross who managed Hawick Farm, this arrangement became increasingly unsustainable.

Neither of Donald's two sons wanted to go into the business, and so decided not to follow in their father's footsteps. Jonathan, who studied chemistry at Nottingham University, has largely worked in the field of medical diagnostics, and is currently Senior Global Product Director with bioMérieux SA, a French multinational biotechnology company. Craig did show some interest in farming, but he finally said to Donald that he did not want to be chasing sheep for the rest of his life. Instead he has found his niche in engineering, developing an expertise in tunnelling machines, and has worked on large tunnelling projects like Eurostar, Crossrail and High Speed 2. He is

---

10. T.J.D. Knight-Jones and J. Rushton, 'The economic impacts of foot and mouth disease – What are they, how big are they and where do they occur?' (*Preventative Veterinary Medicine*, November 2013).

currently Mechanical Superintendent of Hubbway Plant Hire, a large plant hire company.

Although neither Jonathan nor Craig wanted to go into farming, Donald successfully encouraged other young people to realise their ambitions in agriculture. Three young lads whom he employed when they left school – David Brodie, John Charlton and Edward Ridley – were greatly influenced by all the time that he invested in them. They were all from farming families, and so had been deeply involved in farming and had ambitions to farm themselves, but unfortunately there was not enough work on their own family farms for them.

David, for example, took over the sheep flock at Soppit and was able to start his own business when Donald and Rhoda rented Hawick Farm. He was subsequently able to rent a farm on the Wellington Estate, which would have been difficult had he not had the Soppit experience and proved himself capable there. Donald agreed a partnership arrangement with John at Middle Farm when he was spending so much time away from home. John became self-employed, and he, with his wife Fiona, continues to manage his own livestock business and a contracting operation at Middle Farm. Edward used what he had learned with Donald in his future career working for the National Trust.

By the beginning of the new century, because there was no succession, Donald and Rhoda began to slim down the business, giving up the tenancy of Hawick Farm in 2001, until only Middle Farm was left, which they farmed in partnership with John and Fiona Charlton, who finally took over the tenancy after Donald retired from farming in 2018. In his retirement, Donald has remained active in farming politics, and has continued to follow his many interests in the church, the House of Lords and in charitable work.

Looking back at Donald's farming life we can see that he had many successes, but was he right to expand his business as he did? One perhaps thinks of the parable told by Jesus about the rich fool who built more and more barns to hold his increasingly abundant stock of grain. He wanted to *take life easy; eat, drink and be merry*, only for God to say to him, *You fool! This very night your life will be demanded from you. Then who will get what you have prepared for yourself?*[11]

Donald, however, is not like the rich farmer in the parable. For one thing, as we shall see as we explore his life further, he has never taken life easy. His farming life was difficult as he started off with no capital, and he never ended up owning any of the farms, always having rent to pay, along with the interest on borrowed capital. He expanded the business to ensure that the farms were of sufficient size to be viable and efficient.

Besides, the farmer in the parable did not lose his life because of the barns that he built, but because he was *not rich towards God*. Donald, on the other hand, as we shall see, was very much a man of faith.

---

11. Luke 12:13-21

A Man of Faith

Throughout this period of managing his farming business, Donald continued his Christian life as he did as a young man, as we described in the previous chapter. He, Rhoda and the children continued to attend the Brethren fellowship in Thropton, although when they moved to Middle Farm in 1990, Donald and Rhoda decided to join an assembly in Corbridge. Finally, in 2005 they joined Jesmond Parish Church, a large evangelical Anglican church in Newcastle where Rev. David Holloway was the vicar.

Donald was known as an excellent speaker who could clearly and powerfully present the Christian gospel. During his days in the Brethren assemblies, he would preach in different fellowships at least once a month, and many were encouraged and challenged by his clear exposition of the gospel.

He also joined the Scots Gap Male Voice Choir, a choir of sixteen men singing in four-part harmony, organised by Mrs Lizzie Cowan. Everyone called her either Mother (four of her six sons sang in the choir) or Auntie Lizzie, and she kept everyone focused as they practised in her living room each week, looking forward to her famous drop scones. Donald occasionally sang a solo, but modestly he confesses '*not particularly well*'. He and his friend Ossie Johnson were often asked to give a gospel message at the many concerts they gave in rural Northumberland. Indeed Lizzie's own son, Andy, became a Christian through Donald's preaching.[12] The choir was used by God in the

---

12. To read Andy Cowan's description of how he became a Christian, please refer to Jim Cockburn, *Contending for Truth* (Malcolm Down Publishing, 2022), pp. 136-137.

concerts they gave in churches and village halls that were usually full. Donald believed that '*God really blessed that small part of his great work*'.

During their time in farming, Donald and Rhoda never worked on Sundays other than to feed the livestock. This was seen as odd by many looking on, when the sun was shining and the hay was ready to bale or they were in the middle of harvesting silage or, even more importantly, harvesting grain. It was very tempting to work on a Sunday, especially if they were having very poor harvest weather and then a perfect harvest day on a Sunday. They would go off to church and leave the machinery sitting idle in the yard when neighbours were harvesting and taking advantage of the opportunity of fine weather. This was a difficult message for the staff that they employed, and who were anxious to make progress when the weather was good. Donald believed, however, that God would honour their determination to keep the Lord's Day special and that they would not suffer financially for it. Maintaining that standard was important so that they could worship God and be consistent in setting standards for their own family.

The Christian faith that Donald and Rhoda shared enabled them to face many difficulties, whether it was to do with running the farm or with members of their family. As we have mentioned, Jane's disabilities were a real concern to them, and she finally died at the relatively young age of forty-two. Despite her severe disabilities, Jane had nevertheless an amazing personality. Donald had this to say about her:

When Jane was in a humorous mood, she could influence a room. She had the ability to make everybody laugh, because she was laughing. Conversely, if she threw a tantrum, she could have a damaging impact, and nothing was safe, as stuff could fly off the table. Anything in reach was at risk. She could grab some unsuspecting person by the hair. Taking her into a shop was a high risk, as she could grab items off the shelves or she could grab some innocent shopper. We spent lots of time apologising to folks. She knew and recognised people. She displayed affection. I was a big person in her life, and I got lots of cuddles. She was very demonstrative in her own way, and although she could not talk, she could certainly express how she felt.

When Jane was born, Donald and Rhoda had asked themselves the question that most parents who were facing similar circumstances would ask: '*Why is this happening to us?*' Friends of theirs had a baby about the same time, and they announced it in the local newspaper with the verse '*Every good and perfect gift is from above.*'[13] This made them wonder whether Jane was an imperfect gift, and although it took them a while to work through the issues, they understood that everyone is created as an individual with a special place in God's heart. Their initial prayer was for a wonderful and miraculous healing, but they soon learned to pray for strength, good humour, patience and hope to cope with the extra pressures and hard work involved in bringing up Jane. They saw these prayers being answered again and again.

---

13. James 1:17

They knew that God does not make mistakes, and that Jane's life would have a lasting legacy. She had an influence on the lives of many. John Murray recalled that when his and Donald's families went on holiday together, his second daughter, Faye, who was the same age as Jane, spent a lot of time with her and this early experience motivated Faye to go into special needs teaching.

Part of Jane's legacy included the setting up of the charity At Home in the Community, which we shall discuss in a later chapter. When Jane passed away, although it was exceptionally distressing at the time, God gave them peace that his timing is perfect and that they had been very blessed to have had their daughter Jane.

There were two other tragedies that affected Donald and Rhoda. The first took place in May 2000, when Donald lost his brother Stuart in a tragic farming accident at the age of forty-six. Stuart was crushed by a four-wheel-drive loader, the brakes of which had failed. As Donald expressed it:

It was such a tragic experience. Stuart was such a lovely guy, very dedicated, very caring. We all asked why this had happened, because he was needed by his family. He was such an important, stable figure for his wife Margaret and the family. It was a devastating time.

The second tragedy affected Donald's sister Sheena's family, who lived in Edinburgh. On 30th May 2007, Sheena's daughter, Rachel, was coming back home from collecting the children from school and nursery when a four-by-four car tore out of a junction opposite their house, failed to turn the corner and crashed into Rachel and four-year-old Olivia. Tragically, Olivia was killed and Rachel had to have her leg amputated. The car just drove off, but the driver was later apprehended by the police and was discovered to have been high on drugs.

In reflecting upon these tragedies, Donald was able to say:

Everyone goes through dreadful, emotional sadness. It's awful having to face up to these issues; they are never ever forgotten, but are always there. There are reminders all the time of these tragedies that have taken place; whether it's the date in the calendar or birthdays or family gatherings, there is always the sense that these people are missing. I have to rationalise it, and we talk about it as a family. This is a fallen, sinful world, and the tarnishing impact of sin affects every aspect of life. We are not given a special cordon of protection around us. We are subject to the same influences as everybody else in this fallen world. Brakes fail, there are drug-fuelled drivers and Christians are not exempt from the tragedies of life. We need to see ourselves as transitioning through this sinful world, and our destination is more important than the journey. God's will is something we have to accept and subject ourselves to, no matter if it seems that it is an irrational, illogical, tragic waste of life when you experience these things. This is part of God's eternal plan, and where we are going is so much more important than where we are now.

Despite these family tragedies, Donald and Rhoda know that they have been blessed by God in the family that they have been given. They dearly love their sons, Jonathan and

Craig, and their wives, Kate and Sharon, and their children, Eleanor and her husband Joe, Jacob, Zara, Sian and Alex.

The wider Curry family now has more than seventy members, coming from Donald and his four siblings. It is a major event when they all come together, as they do each year on the last Saturday in June for a family day of fun and games on the beach at Longhoughton, and ending with a feast of fish and chips. Family life is very important to Donald, who, as the oldest sibling, enjoys being the patriarch of this large family, giving them advice, encouragement and support. Not all of the family members have a personal Christian faith, but Donald believes that they have all been shaped by Christian values that were passed down from Rob and Barbara Curry. Donald and Rhoda continue to pray for them all.

Donald allowed his faith in God to drive him in all aspects of his life, as we shall see in subsequent chapters.

CHAPTER THREE

North Country Primestock

The Need for Innovation

There is a verse in the letter written by James in the New Testament that uses the patience of the farmer as an example to the rest of us:

> *Be patient, then, brothers and sisters, until the Lord's coming. See how the farmer waits for the land to yield its valuable crop, patiently waiting for the autumn and spring rains.*[14]

Donald was very much like that patient farmer, waiting for the crop or, more likely in his case, his livestock to be ready for market, knowing that it is all in God's hands. He has been known, however, to become rather less patient and even frustrated at inefficient practices within the industry. When Donald sees a problem, he likes to find a solution to make systems work better for the benefit of all concerned. A future colleague of his, Tony Pexton, later said that he

---

14. James 5:7

'*was always interested in being involved in making things better*'. This was to be a driving force in his career.

One early example of his desire to overcome inefficiency came from the time when he worked for his father Rob on the farm at Low Burradon. It concerned the bagging of grain from an early model of combine harvester. When the bags were full, the necks were tied with string, then sent down a chute, until there were three or four, and then a lever was pulled to drop them on to the ground. As Donald explained, '*This was completely daft because all the bags had then to be lifted back up on to trailers afterwards.*' Donald worked with others to design a large platform that was hinged on the side of the combine harvester, level with the bagging area. Up to eight bags could be stacked on the platform. The combine could then drive alongside a trailer, and the bags then quickly lifted straight on to it. This was a simple but ingenious solution.

Later on in his working life, Donald was to face a more complex source of frustration in trying to improve the marketing of livestock products. This became increasingly necessary in the late 1980s when it was clear that the government was going to change the subsidy system, as it finally did in 1990. Subsidies have been traditionally given to farmers to support them in their essential work of providing foodstuffs for the population at reasonable prices. The issue for debate was how that subsidy was applied and distributed to individual farmers.

Prior to the changes made in 1990, the Meat and Livestock Commission was contracted by the government to supply staff, known as graders, to inspect each animal brought to the auction mart or the abattoir to see if they met the standards required to obtain a government subsidy. These graders were not particularly popular because if they rejected an animal, the farmer had to take it back home, and so, in essence, they stood between the farmer and his subsidy cheque. In 1990 the previous system of subsidies determined by grading was abolished, to be replaced by subsidies on breeding stock. This meant that instead of a subsidy being paid when livestock was sent to market, a government grant was paid for each breeding ewe or cow on the farm.

By this time, Donald was increasingly frustrated by the livestock industry's poor approach to marketing their products. To him, it seemed that too many farmers were working towards pleasing the graders in order to receive their subsidy, rather than providing the high-quality meat that the market demanded. Donald felt strongly that farmers should be listening to what the market was saying and responding to changes in consumer demand. This was particularly important at this time as there was growing public concern demonstrated in high-level campaigns over the safety of meat. Animal welfare was becoming a contentious issue, including the treatment of animals both when they were being transported and in abattoirs. The traceability of meat had become an increasing concern as the market demanded absolute transparency as to where it had come from. It seemed that consumer confidence in our food was at an all-time low, and so Donald felt the need for a set of quality standards that would reassure the public.

He was increasingly well known in the livestock industry at national level, and so he was asked to chair an industry working group representing farmers, processors and retailers to draft a farm assurance scheme with a set of standards for livestock on farms. This scheme, called FABBL (Farm Assurance for British Beef and Lamb), led to farms being visited by independent inspectors, enabling farmers to demonstrate that their product had met independently certified standards and so was safe to eat.[15]

FABBL was a major step forward but Donald wanted more; he wanted farmers in the north to work together to meet the standards required.

Forming North Country Primestock

Donald believed that the most effective way for farmers to work together was to form a co-operative, and so he began by meeting with a group of farmers in Northumberland. The aim of the discussions was to see if there could be agreement on changing the way that they, as a group of farmers, marketed their livestock. The timing was right because with the abolition of the grading system, farmers had the opportunity to participate in developing the new quality assurance standards, and this required substantial training. They had to become much more skilled in handling their livestock and in understanding whether they were going to meet the standards or not. Training as a group was clearly more cost effective than farmers individually trying to source their own training. The group agreed to go ahead and form a co-operative. A working

---

15. The FABBL scheme was the forerunner of the Red Tractor scheme that was later introduced in 2000, displaying a red tractor, the Union Jack and a tick to show that the food being sold is of British origin and has been quality assured to certified standards.

group was formed, chaired by Donald, and they went about seeking advice from other groups who had gone through a similar process as well as obtaining legal advice on the constitution of the co-operative.

The organisation started in Northumberland, but it spread westwards to Cumbria and southwards to Durham and North Yorkshire. Donald used his influence to persuade other farmers to join the co-operative by speaking at farmers' meetings and writing in appropriate journals. For example, a full-page article about the new co-operative appeared in *The Grocer* in June 1991, quoting Donald as he put forward his arguments for well-planned marketing, undertaken with integrity to meet consumer demand:

Too many farmers who are content to spend twenty hours a day nursing their ewes and lambs at lambing time and then caring for their flocks throughout the year, simply load their animals on to a lorry and dump them on the market hoping that somebody will be inclined to buy them ... I believe that through efficient marketing and strong promotion we can increase significantly lamb consumption in this country and on the Continent, but producers must be prepared to move with the markets in terms of quality and consistency.[16]

After a lead-in period of about eighteen months, North Country Primestock (NCP) was launched with a fanfare at Kirkley Hall College of Agriculture on Wednesday 17th July 1991. David Curry MP (no relation to Donald), a minister in the Ministry of Agriculture, Food and

---

16. 'An Opportunity for Closer Co-operation' (*The Grocer*, 22nd June 1991).

Fisheries (MAFF), came as the guest speaker praising the new organisation for leading the industry into a *'new era of realism with the emphasis on consistent quality running alongside effective marketing'*.[17]

Donald chaired the board of NCP for about twenty years and was well supported by board members, including John Goodfellow, Nick White, Charles Beaumont and John Murray. From the response of farmers, there seemed to be a real need for such an organisation with all of the changes that were taking place. As a group they were able to negotiate contracts with processors and major retailers such as Tesco, Asda, Waitrose and Marks & Spencer. This gave farmers a degree of countervailing power against the might of the supermarkets in agreeing a price for their products.

For Donald, the underlying rationale behind the co-operative was partnership. In a bid to obtain grant funding from the European Union, the following summary statement was included:

NCP is about partnership, integration and linkage. It links primary producers together in remote areas away from easy markets. It forms partnerships between its members and its customers. It seeks to integrate the industry with the retailer and consumer to bring about the total quality from farm to plate.[18]

---

17. David Leach, 'Farmers entering a new era of realism' (*The Journal,* Saturday 20th July 1991).
18. North Country Primestock, *A Proposal, Feasibility Study and Business Plan to Form a Bid for Funding under EU Objective 5b* (1995), p. 6.

Membership requirements to join NCP were very stringent. Farmers had to agree to have their farms inspected and to comply with all of the assurance standards covering areas such as animal-handling facilities, proper records of animal health, up-to-date transportation records and the storage of pharmaceuticals. Although some farmers did not like the idea of their farms being inspected, Donald believed that having standards that were quality assured and transparent was a much more professional way of marketing stock and meeting the concerns of consumers.

NCP enjoyed a great deal of success in its early years, and huge quantities of livestock were marketed through it. At its peak they marketed about a quarter of a million lambs and about eight thousand cattle a year. It grew to be a substantial business. The business, however, was not without its challenges. One challenge was to find good managers who could bring together the disparate stakeholders involved in the business. The board was very fortunate to find managers and administrators of quality, such as Eric Cooper, Brian Stobo, John Horncastle and Pauline Lishman, who were able to negotiate contracts with processors and supermarkets, ensure that abattoirs awarded fair prices to all member farmers, and deal with grumbling farmers.

The farmers themselves could be a challenge. Some were more trustworthy than others, and some were not particularly skilled in maintaining the quality standards. The co-operative replaced the auction system, and a number of farmers harked back to auction days when they would meet together with their old farming friends; they missed the camaraderie of the mart. Some also mistakenly believed that they could get better prices on their own without the help of the co-operative. Therefore, NCP found that its members varied significantly in their degree of loyalty, ranging from those who marketed their entire output through the company, through those who made a commitment to market a proportion and stuck to it, and to those who looked upon NCP as just another market outlet. Keeping member farmers on board and satisfied was at times a very difficult job for the managers of NCP.

The Demise of North Country Primestock

What started out as a pioneering, even transformative approach to livestock marketing, however, finally failed. This was a great disappointment to Donald but, as he philosophically put it, *'The agricultural world is littered with failed co-operatives, and eventually this one did fail.'* Donald had stepped down as Chair of the board about two years before it went into liquidation. He sometimes wonders if he had stayed on as Chair whether NCP might have survived. There had, however, been mistakes made, which in conjunction with the disloyalty of some members, as mentioned above, brought down the business.

One unfortunate misjudgement was the purchase of an abattoir in Lincoln in 2002. This particular abattoir was relatively small and it had no meat-processing facilities. The slaughtered carcasses had to be sent to an abattoir in South Wales that had processing facilities to provide meat for Tesco, who bought all of NCP's produce from the abattoir. This in itself was a considerable distance, but it was compounded by the fact that the slaughtered animals suffered shrinkage on the journey and thus lost value. The profit margin was thus greatly reduced by transporting the carcasses over such a long distance. Furthermore, in the 1990s, as a result of the BSE crisis, offal from the slaughtered animal had to be removed and destroyed before the animal could be transported. This was a significant cost for small abattoirs such as the NCP abattoir at Lincoln, and again their profit margin was significantly eaten into. The abattoir ended up making serious losses, and it was finally closed in 2004. Its failure contributed to the final downfall of NCP.

Looking back, Donald feels that they were naïve and should have known better than to buy such a small abattoir without processing facilities on-site. Likewise, he felt that they should have been more resilient in facing financial shocks. They had some bad debtors, mainly small businesses that could not pay the money they owed NCP, and unfortunately NCP did not have trade insurance cover for the debts of these small businesses (although they had cover for larger customers). NCP should not have traded with companies for which it could not get bad debt insurance cover.

Perhaps what is more surprising, given the problems that it faced, is that the business lasted as long as it did. Over the years of its operation, the co-operative undertook strategic reviews, and there was a consistent concern about its low profitability and weak balance sheet.

As a result, finally, after twenty-five years, the organisation that had started off with a great fanfare had run out of cash, and so NCP went into liquidation in 2016. Donald had used his considerable energy and entrepreneurial skills to set something up for the benefit of both farmers and consumers. He is aware of mistakes that were made, and how at times they lost sight of the co-operative's original principles of maintaining a strong partnership with retailers and processors. He does not, however, regret trying to bring greater professionalism and transparency to the livestock market, and for this his efforts should be remembered.

James, from whose New Testament letter we quoted at the beginning of this chapter, gave these warnings against being presumptuous in business:

> *Now listen, you who say, 'Today or tomorrow we will go to this or that city, spend a year there, carry on business and make money.' Why, you do not even know what will happen tomorrow. What is your life? You are a mist that appears for a little while and then vanishes. Instead, you ought to say, 'If it is the Lord's will, we will live and do this or that.' As it is, you boast in your arrogant schemes. All such boasting is evil.'[19]*

Donald has always been aware that he has not been guaranteed success in all of his business ventures, and whatever success he has had is not a matter for arrogant boasting, but rather it is all the result of the Lord's will. In the case of North Country Primestock, the Lord brought it to a conclusion, and Donald, although very disappointed about its demise, accepted that gracefully.

19. James 4:13-16

PART TWO

Looking Outward

CHAPTER FOUR

The National Farmers' Union

First Forays into Agricultural Politics

Much of Donald's life has been spent dealing with political issues related to the world of agriculture, working with government in order to improve the state of the industry for the benefit of both consumers and producers. This involved him, amongst other things, heading up government commissions, leading the response to crises in the industry, producing influential reports and serving as a peer in the House of Lords. His first experience of delving into this new world came through the National Farmers' Union (NFU).

The NFU was formed in 1908 when a group of farmers came together at the Smithfield Show in London to discuss whether they could form a national association to represent the interest of farmers. This was a time of particular difficulty for the industry as it faced a period of depression with cheap foodstuffs coming in from overseas. There had been earlier attempts to form an agricultural union, representing all who belonged to the industry, including landlords, tenant and owner-occupying farmers and agricultural workers, but because of conflicting interests amongst the various groups, these attempts were unsuccessful. The NFU emerged as a body representing tenant and owner-occupying farmers, with agricultural workers joining the NUAW (National Union of Agricultural Workers) and landlords joining the CLBA (Country Land and Business Association). As such, the NFU is not really a trade union in the sense of a body bargaining with employers for higher wages, threatening sanctions in order to achieve them; rather, it is a professional association that lobbies government to produce policies of benefit to the industry.

Donald's father Rob was a member of the Rothbury branch in Northumberland, and when Donald was working for him on the family farm at Low Burradon, he would accompany him to NFU meetings. When Donald and Rhoda moved to Kirkharle, David Scales, the NFU Group Secretary for East Northumberland, persuaded him to join the Cambo branch. Donald found the meetings interesting, especially the debates on government policy development and proposed legislation affecting the farming sector. After two or three years, David persuaded Donald to allow his name to be put forward as Chair of the Cambo branch. He was duly elected, and then later became a member of the Northumberland county branch committee. All of this was giving Donald useful experience in committee work, which would be of vital experience in the future.

He was asked on a number of occasions if he would allow his name to be put forward to become Chair of the county branch, but each time he declined. The role involved social responsibilities, such as attending dinners and other functions, as well as organising an annual dinner dance. Donald was not really interested in this element of the role, particularly as it would mean leaving Rhoda to look after Jane on her own for a number of evenings in the week. He also felt that the business was still in a fragile state, and so he needed to give it his full attention.

NFU National Council

As we mentioned in chapter two, by the time Jane reached the age of fourteen Donald and Rhoda found it increasingly difficult to look after her at home, and so they made the heart-rending decision to place Jane in residential care in Stelling Hall. This gave Donald a greater freedom to be involved in the work of the NFU.

In 1985 he was persuaded to be one of two delegates to represent Northumberland on the NFU National Council, replacing Denny Spence, a good friend and a successful farmer from Fourstones near Hexham. The other delegate at the time was Arthur Gray from Broomhill, who was a highly respected farmer and who acted as a mentor to Donald, guiding him into the world of national agricultural politics. On the train journey down to London for his first council meeting, John Moor, who farmed near Sunderland, introduced him to Ben Gill, who boarded the train at York and was also attending his first council meeting. He and Ben worked together on a number of committees and became great friends. Ben eventually became President of the NFU from 1998 to 2004. Ben was just one of the many interesting people that Donald met through his NFU work, people that Donald described as *'honest, genuine, upright, hardworking farmers, the salt of the earth who cared deeply about their fellow farmers and wanted to make a difference'.*

Much of the work on the council was done in committees, and Donald was appointed to the livestock and wool committee, the cereals committee and the marketing committee. Donald found the work on these committees and the council as a whole fascinating, and was his first real exposure to being able to influence policy making. He always ensured that he reported council discussions back to the Northumberland branch.

The 1980s was a decade of insecurity for the industry, with fluctuations in currency markets, high interest rates and bad publicity in terms of butter and grain mountains and the ploughing up of hedgerows. In addition, a completely unexpected crisis for the sheep industry occurred as a result of nuclear fallout from the Chernobyl disaster of 1986, with residues of nuclear iodine found in lamb meat due to grazing pastures being polluted by the fallout. Approximately ten thousand farms across the United Kingdom faced restrictions on animal movement that year due to the fallout, and many continued to do so for years to come. These areas of concern were discussed in committee and full council meetings. Donald endeavoured to ensure that the voice of Northumberland was heard and the needs of Northumberland farmers appreciated, rather than be drowned out by the greater numbers of southern farmers. His was seen as the voice of reason, trying to get agriculture, and particularly northern agriculture, understood.

The influence of the NFU lay in its lobbying power with government, working with government ministers for the benefit of the farming community. The key person in negotiations from the NFU side was the President of the NFU. Donald got to know each of the Presidents well. The first President that he came into contact with was Henry Plumb, whom Donald heard when he spoke at a Northumberland NFU Annual General Meeting. Donald described him as *'an inspiring speaker, very articulate with a great grasp of political issues'* and *'regarded as having been the greatest NFU President'*. He was knighted and when he stood down from the NFU, he became a Member of the European Parliament, and indeed its only ever United Kingdom President. On retiring from the European Parliament, Sir Henry became a member of the House of Lords, and would later be one of Donald's supporters when he himself was introduced into the Lords in October 2011. Lord Plumb died in 2022, and Clarence House asked Donald if he would represent Prince Charles at the memorial service in November of that year. By that time, however, Queen Elizabeth had died, and so in effect Donald ended up representing the monarch at Lord Plumb's memorial service, which Donald described as *'a huge honour'*.

Donald could have decided to try to obtain high office in the NFU like Henry Plumb, Ben Gill and other influential figures within the union, but he felt that that was not the road that God was leading him down. In 1987 he got an opportunity to take a senior role on the council when the position of Vice-Chair of the livestock and wool committee became vacant. His friend Ben Gill offered to support him and not stand against him. Other members of the committee encouraged him to stand and offered to lobby for him. Nevertheless, Donald declined to stand. One reason was financial: it was a three-day week commitment without any financial support, and Donald could not afford that. The other reason was that if Donald were to step on that ladder, he felt that he would be indicating that he was committing to an NFU ambition that he did not want to undertake. Ben Gill took on the position of Vice-Chair of that committee, and then finally rose to become NFU President. As Donald said, '*It was a defining moment for him and for me.*'

In 1992 Donald was appointed Deputy Chair of the Meat and Livestock Commission (MLC), and, as we shall see in the next chapter, a year later he went on to chair the commission. He felt that his MLC appointment could lead to a conflict of interests with his membership of the NFU National Council, and so in that year he stood down from the council.

NFU Mutual

From small beginnings when it was formed by seven farmers in a tea shop in Stratford-upon-Avon in 1910, NFU Mutual has become the largest rural insurer, and has developed an excellent service for the farming community and other rural businesses from hauliers to butcher shops. NFU and NFU Mutual are separate organisations, but they are linked through their group secretaries (the NFU term) and their agents (the NFU Mutual term), who are usually one and the same person. When David Scales came to Kirkharle to persuade Donald to join the NFU, he also wanted to check that Donald was insured with NFU Mutual. Being an agent for NFU Mutual provides the income for the NFU group secretaries.

As he became more widely known on the national agricultural scene through his involvement with the NFU and the MLC, members of the board of NFU Mutual began to take an increasingly strong interest in Donald, and sought to enlist his services. In 1997 he was invited to speak on the work of the Meat and Livestock Commission at a dinner held by the board of NFU Mutual at their head office in Stratford-upon-Avon. Unbeknown to him, he was actually being assessed by the board with a view to possible board membership. He passed whatever clandestine test they had, and was invited to join the board.

Donald obviously knew a lot about agriculture, but he knew nothing at all about the financial services sector. He was invited to spend a day at their head office on an induction course. A day was, however, barely adequate to get to grips with what was a very complex company, and Donald felt that it was a year before he could make meaningful contributions to board meetings. Nevertheless, Donald felt that it was a huge privilege to be involved with such a successful organisation with such excellent staff.

In 2001 he became Vice-Chair and two years later he was elected Chair. One of the first things that he did as Chair was to establish a more professional induction programme for new board members to replace the inadequate programme that he had gone through. He also introduced an annual appraisal process for board members, together with an annual review of board performance, often involving an independent assessor. The Financial Services Authority complimented the company for having what were, at the time, industry-leading induction and appraisal processes.

There was a large volume of work associated with chairing the monthly meetings of the board; the volume of papers produced required about two days of intensive reading, as they contained often very complex financial analysis. Because of the close link between the NFU and NFU Mutual through the secretary and agent roles, Donald and his Chief Executive also spent time in meetings with the NFU President and Director General.

At the turn of the century, the board was under immense pressure to demutualise, which would have meant that members would no longer own the company. The company was particularly vulnerable to attack as it had a very strong balance sheet, which would provide large financial rewards to those who would become shareholders in a demutualised company. Standing up against demutualisation seemed the right approach as many other companies that had demutualised had either failed or been swallowed up by larger corporations; Donald did not want NFU Mutual to lose its personal identity and the close ties it had with its members.

Donald's time as Chair coincided with periods of upheaval in financial services, with a financial downturn in 2003–2004 and the banking crisis of 2007–2008. Solvency ratios and investment policies had to be carefully scrutinised, and Donald and the Chief Executive were regularly called to meetings with the Financial Services Authority (FSA) regulator in Canary Wharf, so that the regulator could be assured that the organisation was able to withstand financial shocks. NFU Mutual came through these crises well, as its reserves were strong and able to face the vicissitudes of the markets. Financial reserves were important for mutual companies because they could not just go to the stock market to get funding, as all their funding came from their members.

Donald was also involved in other areas in leading the company. For example, a risk management company was set up to support farmers and other businesses by reviewing the risks they faced in areas such as health and safety and thus helping them to reduce their risk exposure. He was also responsible for leading the appointment of senior staff and recruiting new board members who each had to be approved by the FSA. One of his appointments was a new Chief Executive, Lindsay Sinclair, who previously worked for Dutch bank IMG. By making this appointment, Donald showed his usual independence of mind because he broke the company tradition of only appointing homegrown chief executives rather than recruiting fresh talent from other companies.

The company celebrated its centenary in 2010, and Donald, who was due to retire as Chair the previous year, was asked to remain in office to lead the centenary celebrations. The main event was to be a formal celebration dinner at the offices of the Institute of Directors in London, to which Donald had invited one hundred and sixty guests. Unfortunately, Donald himself was not able to attend the dinner as he was lying in a hospital bed. The day before the dinner, he felt an odd sensation in his stomach, and so after going to a walk-in centre (on Rhoda's advice), he was told to go to St Thomas's Hospital. He took the bus (to Rhoda's surprise), and on being admitted he was diagnosed with appendicitis, and operated on that day. The dinner itself went very well, despite Donald's unavoidable absence.

Donald finally stepped down from the board in 2011 after fourteen enjoyable years with the company. Just before he retired, he toured the regional offices to thank staff for their support. He received generous gifts from the staff, including Scotch whisky, Irish whiskey, Welsh whisky and English whisky. As he himself commented, '*I have no idea what made them all think that I was a whisky drinker.*'

He also received from the board a bound volume of tributes written by each board member. The following is part of one of these tributes (given in this case by Steve Bower), which is typical of the comments made by board members:

> *You embody our values and have been a vocal champion of mutuality, our unique agency network and the close links with the farming industry that makes us so unique and successful. You also have a great personal touch, making anyone you speak to feel that they have your complete attention. Our founders would have seen your position as Chairman in our centenary year as being absolutely fitting and true to the vision they established one hundred years ago.*

Why This Man?

In serving the NFU and NFU Mutual, Donald took on increasingly responsible positions. We see a man who was strongly encouraged by his colleagues to take on these roles, and he won the support of many in the industry as he represented their interests. Sometimes, however, he stood back and would not let himself be pushed into roles that he did not believe were right for him at the time, as was the case when Northumberland colleagues repeatedly asked him to chair the county branch. Likewise, when senior council members such as Ben Gill wanted him to become Vice-Chair of the livestock and wool committee, he declined, even though it might well have led him ultimately to becoming NFU President.

So what was it about this man that made both ordinary farmers and highly esteemed members of the NFU Council want him to be their representative? When we look at Donald what we see are his complete honesty and integrity, his understanding of and love for the agricultural community, his attention to detail and his eloquence. People trusted Donald absolutely; he would listen to their concerns and act accordingly.

One of those who worked closely with Donald on the NFU Council was Glen Sanderson, another delegate who represented Northumberland and who would later become Leader of Northumberland County Council. He is full of admiration for Donald:

Don is a very special person. I have come across lots of excellent people in my work over the years, but Don Curry is in the top five. When reporting back to the Northumberland branch meeting, he always displayed a complete grasp of his subject. I have never heard him swear, lose his temper or say an unkind word to anyone. He was the voice of reason, but he was also good fun, never boring.

Meurig Raymond was a former NFU President who knew Donald well, and again he admired his integrity and depth of knowledge about agriculture. He saw Donald as *'the go-to person for advice'*. He knew that Donald was a Christian, but *'although he was a true believer, he did not force his Christianity on anyone'*. When Ben Gill died in 2014, Meurig, who was President at the time, recalled the eulogy that Donald gave at the funeral, saying that it was *'the best ever'*, and how *'Donald's Christian beliefs helped him through'*. In February 2025, Meurig invited Donald to an award ceremony where he was presented with the National Arable and Grassland Outstanding Achievement Award, saying, *'With over forty years of dedicated service to farming families this Award is so very well deserved.'*

When the apostle Paul wrote to the church in Thessalonica, it was clear that he admired the way that they were living for Jesus. He said this:

> *We always thank God for all of you and continually mention you in our prayers. We remember before our God and Father your work produced by faith, your labour prompted by love, and your endurance inspired by hope in our Lord Jesus Christ.*[20]

People could see these qualities in Donald. His hard work, endurance and concern for people all stem from his relationship with God; he had a faith in God, a love for

20. 1 Thessalonians 1:2-3

Jesus, and a hope in Jesus that would take him through to eternity. These spiritual qualities enabled him to serve others so effectively, and we shall continue to see these qualities at work in future chapters.

CHAPTER FIVE

The Meat and Livestock Commission

Into the Public Eye

If the National Farmers' Union gave Donald his first taste of agricultural politics and his first involvement in the national agricultural scene, it would be the Meat and Livestock Commission (MLC) that would catapult him into the public eye. This was largely a result of the crises that hit agriculture in the 1990s. These crises, particularly outbreaks of livestock disease, would bring Donald into direct contact not only with farmers but also consumers, retailers and government itself. These were frenzied times, and his God-given qualities of diplomacy, depth of thought and ability to communicate would be well used in his service as a commissioner.

The MLC had been established in 1967 as a public body with commissioners appointed by the government of the day. In its fortieth anniversary annual report, it described its remit as:

to work with the British meat and livestock industry (cattle, sheep and pigs) to improve its efficiency and competitive position; and to maintain and stimulate markets for red meat at home and British meat abroad, with due regard for the consumer.[21]

In 1967, when the commission was set up, it was recognised that sectors in agriculture needed help, particularly in areas of research and promotion. To pay for this assistance, levy boards were established for the different sectors. In the case of the MLC, levies were paid at the point of slaughter; the farmer paid seventy-five per cent of the levy per animal and the abattoir paid the remaining twenty-five per cent (although these proportions varied over time). Inevitably, both farmers and the abattoirs complained about these payments, but without them the MLC could not carry out the research and promotion that it was commissioned to do in the best interests of both farmers and consumers.

Regional boards of the MLC were also established, and in 1980 Donald was appointed to the North Regional Board. This gave him a useful introduction to the workings of the MLC, and he found the North Regional Manager, Iain Hall, a great support to him in these early days. He also gained himself a reputation as a bit of a rebel, as he often challenged decisions made or the quality of the promotional materials produced for the different sectors.

A change took place in 1986. There was in existence a body called the Meat Promotion Executive (MPE) that was

---

21. Meat and Livestock Commission, *Annual Report and Accounts* (2007), p. 3.
     This particular report happened to be its last as a separate body, as in 2007 it was subsumed into the Agriculture and Horticulture Development Board, as part of government rationalisation.

semi-autonomous from the MLC. There was some tension between the two bodies as they had some overlapping roles, and so it was finally decided to abolish the MPE. In its place, three new promotion bodies were created, positioned within the MLC framework. They were the Beef Promotion Council, the Lamb Promotion Council and the Pork and Bacon Promotion Council, each of them chaired by farmers. Donald was asked to chair the Lamb Promotion Council. In addition, three additional farmers were appointed to the board of the MLC. By this time Donald was well known through his work on the North Regional Board, and so it was no surprise that he was appointed to the MLC board on 1st October 1986.

His main priority in his work with the Lamb Promotion Council was to reverse the declining consumption of British lamb. One reason for this decline was the fallout from the Chernobyl disaster of 1986, which we mentioned in the previous chapter. Donald worked closely with the media as they developed advertising campaigns that would encourage consumers to eat more lamb. The most notable campaign took place at the end of the 1980s and the beginning of the 1990s, and was called 'Slam in the Lamb',[22] and starred Geoffrey Palmer, well known to viewers of television situation comedies at the time such as *The Fall and Rise of Reginald Perrin* and *Butterflies*. Advertisements were also made for Belgian television. The campaigns were deemed effective in that lamb consumption per head rose in the late '80s and early '90s. Donald wrote in an article in *Farmers' Weekly* where he boldly stated, '*We must regard the past ten years as a great success story for the British sheep*

---

22.   https://www.youtube.com/watch?v=9bcIRV2yaHE (accessed 24.10.23).

industry.'[23] Lamb consumption per head would, however, return to its downward trend as the effectiveness of the campaigns wore off and people continued to eat more processed foods.[24]

Chair of the MLC

In 1992 Donald was appointed Deputy Chair of the MLC, which he saw as a great honour. It actually came through as he lay on the operating table recovering from surgery in December 1991.

Donald had developed a problem with his left leg and arm: his toes and the ends of his fingers were numb; he lost the ability to do anything with his left arm and he was dragging his left foot. It started in the lambing season in 1991 when he found that he was not able to chase after sheep, and the problem intensified as the year went on. He sought medical advice, but nobody seemed to know what was causing the problem or what could be done about it. A doctor friend of his, however, seemed to believe that it was serious and that he should consult a neurologist straight away.

On admission to hospital a consultant told him that he had a non-malignant meningioma tumour that was gradually compressing his spinal cord. He was prepared for surgery, and before the operation, his surgeon, Alistair Jenkins, had asked Donald what he did. Donald explained that he was a livestock farmer and a Commissioner for the Meat and

---

23. Donald Curry 'Talking Politics' (*Farmers' Weekly, 3rd February 1990*).
24. Cesar Revoredo-Ghia 'The British are eating less red meat and consuming more processed food' (*LSE Business Review, 2021*).

Livestock Commission. Mr Jenkins then confessed that he was a vegetarian. Despite the seriousness of the situation, Donald maintained his sense of humour and said to Mr Jenkins, '*You're asking me, a farmer who produces meat and is a board member of the Meat and Livestock Commission, to put my life in the hands of a vegetarian?*' To which Mr Jenkins replied, '*Yes!*'

The surgery was considered to be high risk due to the close proximity of the tumour to the brain and the spinal cord. Mr Jenkins actually asked Donald and Rhoda if they had put their house in order because of the very high risk of failure. Donald, however, was quite relaxed about it and believed that God was in control. The operation was successful and Mr Jenkins was able to extract a tumour about the size of a golf ball. He told Donald that if nothing had been done, he would only have had three weeks before the tumour would have stopped his breathing and his lungs would collapse. As he was recovering in the High Dependency Unit, there was concern that such a delicate operation could possibly result in brain damage. Mr Jenkins asked Donald how he felt, to which Donald replied, '*I feel as if I have been attacked by a Scottish vegetarian.*' It was clear that Donald's mental faculties were absolutely fine!

Mr Jenkins, however, was not yet finished with Donald as he believed that Donald would be an excellent case study to discuss with medical students, and so a few weeks later, Donald was asked if he would present himself at a seminar in the Royal Victoria Infirmary in Newcastle to be questioned by medical students. Donald continued to be used in this way for about two years.

After his recuperation from the operation, he took up his new post as Deputy Chair. This was an excellent introduction to the role that he would take on in a year's time when he would have full responsibility as Chair. The current Chair was Geoffrey John, who came to the MLC from United Biscuits where he had gained lots of experience in chairing board meetings. Donald learned a lot from Geoffrey. In July 1993, however, Geoffrey decided to relinquish his role with the MLC when he took up two new appointments as Chair of Food from Britain and Chair of Dairy Crest.

Because Donald was Deputy Chair, he was expected to take on the role of Acting Chair on Geoffrey's resignation. Donald was happy to do this, provided that they appointed a permanent Chair very soon. Richard Packer, Permanent Secretary at the Ministry of Agriculture, Fisheries and Food (MAFF), told him, '*You don't have to take any serious decisions. Just keep the show on the road until we find a new Chair.*' This, however, did not reflect Donald's attitude to his responsibilities, as he was never the person who wanted just to '*keep the show on the road*'. Donald replied, '*You had better find someone else then. I am not taking this on unless I can take serious decisions. There is an urgent and substantial restructuring job to be done that might include redundancies, and I am not taking on the Chair unless I have the authority to take action.*' Richard Packer conceded to Donald's demands.

Over the next nine months he continued as Acting Chair and carried out the necessary restructuring. The government was looking for an independent Chair, in the belief that someone who had no ties to agriculture would not be biased or be under undue influence from any part of the industry, and so would be able to act or think independently. Such a person may, however, have no real understanding of the industry or the sensitivities of different groups within the industry. For whatever reason, MAFF had not found a permanent Chair nine months after Donald took on the acting role. By this time Donald had lost patience with his ministerial bosses, and so he called Richard Packer on the telephone and said rather bluntly, *'Time's up! You have had nine months and you need to make a decision. Either appoint me or find someone else quickly.'* Ten days later he received a letter from MAFF confirming his appointment as Chair of the Meat and Livestock Commission as from 1st April 1994.[25]

Donald found his role within the MLC fascinating, but it was hard work. Skilful negotiation had to take place with a large number of interest groups if, for example, they wanted to change a levy. There were also perceived dangers associated with the job, such as death threats from farmers who felt that the levy system worked against their interests. Also in the early '90s, the Animal Liberation Front were using violence to get their message across, and Special Branch believed that Donald was one of their principal targets. Officers visited their home to discuss security issues with Donald and Rhoda, including installing surveillance cameras, looking out for mysterious parcels and checking the underside of the car before making a journey. (Rhoda had to confess that she did not know what the underside of the car should look like!)

---

25. Gwyn Howells, who was Director General at the time of Donald's retirement, recalls Donald saying at his leaving function, *'I was Acting Chairman for so long that I became a member of Equity.'*

He liked to visit groups across the country to deal with the concerns they had. Each year he embarked on a programme of regional visits to meet the levy payers. Donald regarded it as essential to have face-to-face opportunities to explain what the Commission was doing, how the levy was being spent for the benefit of the industry and dealing with any issues that concerned them.

On one occasion, Meurig Raymond, later to become NFU President, invited Donald to a meeting of farmers in Pembrokeshire, where there were many dissenting voices against the MLC and the levy grading system. About a hundred and twenty angry farmers were gathered at the meeting, venting their fury at how much the MLC cost them, and whether it was of any benefit to them. Meurig recalled the meeting saying:

There was a lot of ranting and shouting, but Don, helped by the Chair Denzil Jenkins, handled the meeting very well. He reassured the audience that they were there for the livestock industry. It was amazing how Don was able to calm the meeting down. He is a real gentleman, with such a diplomatic mind; he is top of the league for diplomacy.

Donald recalls attending another meeting in Wales, where he received a number of challenges about what the MLC was allegedly doing or failing to do to help farmers. One farmer got up and asked, '*Mr Curry, am I right in thinking that you have a responsibility to advise the Minister?*' Donald replied, '*That's correct.*' The farmer then said, '*Well, if you don't mind me saying so, I think that you have done a bad job of it*' (expletive removed). Donald quick wittedly replied,

*'It's true that I have a responsibility to advise the Minister,
but the Minister is under no obligation to accept my advice.'*

There was much to discuss in board meetings during
his period as Chair, which was a very challenging one
for the agricultural sector. Overall there continued to be
increasing public disquiet about the quality of food, arising
from disturbing media coverage about bad practice in
abattoirs. Margins in abattoirs were very tight and so there
was little money available to put into improving facilities
or undertaking staff training. Abattoirs had forty-five per
cent overcapacity, and so plans were devised to reduce this
overcapacity and thus stem losses in the industry.

There were other areas of major challenge for the industry
throughout the 1990s. As a result of pressure from the
European Union, the Milk Marketing Board, a national co-
operative organisation selling milk on behalf of all dairy
farmers regardless of the size of herd, was abolished in
1994; it was considered to be a monopoly and so not acting
in the best interest of consumers. As a result of the Barnes
Review, the government also cut back on agricultural
research by privatising the Agricultural Development
Advisory Service in 1997, which meant that farmers were
no longer entitled to free advice based on the latest research.
Demonstration farms, established to allow farmers to see
best practice at first hand, were closed down. All of these
issues were matters of concern to everyone in the industry,
and so their implications were regularly discussed in MLC
board meetings.

Donald had developed his skills in chairing meetings
as a committee Chair with the NFU, and by observing

the chairing strategies of people such as Geoffrey John. Throughout his time as Chair of the MLC, he was seen as a very effective Chair, handling people who had strong views on contentious issues. Although he encouraged debate, he was able to prevent arguments from simply going round in circles and leading nowhere. Instead, he sought to bring arguments to a conclusion. He developed a reputation in meetings of drawing conclusions but without undermining anyone who held a different opinion. He saw himself as a consensus-building Chair, wanting members to come to an amicable agreement, but if he felt that arguments were not going in the right direction, he would not hesitate to intervene to steer the discussion back in the way that he felt it should be going. If a member brought up a contentious issue, Donald would try to reach agreement with the member outside of the meeting, and then bring a resolution back to the meeting. A measure of his success in this was that he never had to rely on a majority vote to pass a resolution through the board.

Much of his effectiveness in chairing was due to the fact that he always did his homework, accumulating detailed knowledge of topics, and understanding the implications and consequences of the issues that were being debated. It was also due to the fact that he knew the members, directors and other staff well. Bob Bansback, Corporate Strategy Director at the MLC, saw how well he handled people both within and beyond meetings:

He had the trust of everyone. He had an amazing knowledge of individuals and took a personal interest in them and their families. He was popular with the staff; he knew their names and was always friendly towards them and smiled at them when he met them.

Sue Walker, his personal assistant, saw him as *'gentle'* and *'a delight to work for'* and was accustomed to receiving calls from Donald as he sat on his combine harvester or *'even while going through a car wash'.*

There was one issue, however, more than any other that would test the mettle of Donald as Chair and his ability to lead the organisation. The issue that totally dominated discussion within the MLC and the industry as a whole was livestock disease, particularly BSE. All of his skills of chairmanship, diplomacy and negotiation would be required as he tackled this major farming crisis. He also knew that he needed God's resources in seeing him through this intense time of difficulty, as he in his own strength felt so inadequate. As he navigated through the crisis, he would later say, as David said in the Old Testament, *'Surely God is my help; the Lord is the one who sustains me.'*[26]

The Plague on Livestock

One of the earliest uses of the term 'plague on livestock' comes in the Old Testament account of how Pharaoh refused to let the Israelites leave Egypt. God sent plagues on the Egyptians, one of which was a 'plague on livestock' that caused the death of all of the Egyptians' (but not the Israelites') cattle, sheep and other animals. This was

26. Psalm 54:4

85

devastating for the ordinary Egyptian farmers who had no idea of what was happening.[27]

In the 1980s and '90s, a plague befell livestock in the United Kingdom and in many cattle-rearing countries across the world. Some cattle seemed to be displaying strange behaviour in the way they walked, as if they had lost control of their muscles; others were aggressive, or excessively nervous. Not long after the cattle displayed such symptoms, they would go into a coma and die. Just as the ancient Egyptian farmers had no idea why the plague on their livestock was happening, modern British farmers also were at a loss to understand what was happening. (It should be said that nobody was suggesting that the British farmers were objects of divine punishment!) This was devastating for the livestock industry, and they looked to government scientists and, of course, the Meat and Livestock Commission for support and answers.

The scientific experts initially did not really understand what was causing this disease. When, however, they examined the brains of dead cattle that seemed to have caught it, they recognised it as a neurodegenerative disease resulting in the neurons in the brain losing their function. The disease became known as 'bovine spongiform encephalopathy' (BSE) or in common parlance, 'mad cow disease'. It is now accepted that the disease comes from a protein known as prion protein that mutated into a harmful form that damages the central nervous system of cattle. The harmful protein causes small holes to be formed in the brain, giving it the form of a sponge. This protein

27. Exodus 9:1-7

was likely to have been contained in meat-and-bone meal that had not been adequately rendered and was then fed to young calves. It took about five years before the symptoms were evident in cattle, a long incubation period that had made the initial diagnosing of the disease and its causes more difficult for the scientific experts.

According to the Centers for Disease Control and Prevention, an American research organisation, the peak of the BSE crisis in the United Kingdom came in January 1993 with almost one thousand new cases per week. In 1995 there were 14,562 cases over the whole year, which fell to 1,443 cases five years later, and by 2015 there were only two cases reported. By the end of 2015 over 184,500 cases had been confirmed since the disease was first diagnosed. More than 35,000 cattle herds had been affected.[28]

These livestock losses were of course disastrous for the farmers concerned, but everyone in the industry was affected by the loss of consumer confidence in meat products. The situation was made much worse in 1996 when it was discovered that the same mutated prion protein that caused BSE in cattle also caused Variant Creutzfeldt-Jacob disease (vCJD), which is a fatal disease in humans. Despite devastating predictions by some scientists that hundreds of thousands would die, it is now recognised that very few cases of CJD, if any, were related to beef consumption, as there was very little evidence of transmission of the disease from cattle to humans.[29] Nevertheless, at the time fear gripped the market for beef products, and it plunged

28. https://www.cdc.gov/prions/bse/index.html (accessed 9/11/23).
29. https://www.mayoclinic.org/diseases-conditions/creutzfeldt-jakob-disease/symptoms-causes/syc-20371226 (accessed 9/11/23).

downward almost overnight when consumers perceived that they too could die from mad cow disease by eating burgers. Unsurprisingly, it was not only domestic sales that were affected; the export market also collapsed. The European Union placed an almost immediate ban in March 1996 on beef exports from the United Kingdom. Prior to the ban, exports represented thirty per cent of all beef produced in the United Kingdom, and so a ban on exports further massively damaged an already struggling industry.[30]

Speaking at the Royal Highland Show in Edinburgh in July 1996, Donald said,

The announcement three months ago by the Health Secretary about the possible link between beef and CJD in humans caused the biggest collapse in consumer confidence in the history of the beef industry[31] . . . Mince sales are down by forty per cent, and they used to account for forty per cent of total sales.[32]

In these crisis years, the farming industry looked to the MLC for help, and Donald and Commission staff worked with the government to introduce measures to try to eradicate the disease. Cattle feed containing any ingredients originating from cattle or sheep was banned. What was termed 'Specified Bovine Material' (the brain, eyes, spinal cord, tonsils, thymus, spleen and intestines) had to be removed from all cattle and destroyed, regardless of whether they showed signs of BSE or not. Only cattle less than thirty months old could enter the food chain,

30. 'BSE Update' (*MLC Bulletin,* July 1996).
31. 'Beef Crisis' (*The Daily Telegraph,* 21st June 1996).
32. 'MLC pushes mince with new standard' (*Farmers' Weekly,* 28th June 1996).

as it was assumed that thirty months was well within the incubation period, and BSE would not have developed in these animals. Compensation was paid to farmers whose cattle were slaughtered under the thirty-month-plus cattle slaughter scheme.

After the 1997 election that returned a Labour government under Tony Blair, Jack Cunningham became Minister of Agriculture, Fisheries and Food. One of his first actions was to introduce a ban on meat on the bone, as the BSE agent had been found in the lymph glands of cattle attached to the bones. Donald, however, felt that this was an overreaction on the part of the government; with the restrictions already in place, there would only be a tiny number of animals incubating the disease. 'A sledgehammer to crack a very small nut,' was how Donald described this particular measure.

Donald was very much in the frontline during this crisis as the face of the MLC. He had a team of experienced directors supporting him and giving excellent advice. Donald did not claim to be an expert in veterinary science, but he had a highly experienced Director General in Colin Maclean, who was a former veterinary surgeon, and Colin was able to provide technical advice to the Commission. Donald felt that it was his role to explain complex scientific analysis to the industry and the general public, and to reassure them that although the issues were serious, measures were being put in place to eradicate the disease. Therefore he spent a lot of time giving media interviews, going from television studios to press conferences, explaining what action the Commission was taking to deal with the crisis and returning the industry to normality. He also attended many farmers' meetings, where he had to reassure farmers that the Commission was working in their best interests. As we have mentioned above, farmers were often hostile to the MLC, but Donald was able to provide a calming influence; farmers trusted Donald because they saw that he was one of their own stock. Bob Bansback pointed out:

> *His relationship with Ben Gill, President of the NFU, was particularly important, because historically MLC had not always got on with NFU leaders. He was very close to Ben, and that was important for us because Ben was such a dominant figure.*

His Marketing Director, Gwyn Howells, gave advice on how best to promote the sales of British beef once it seemed that the disease was under control. There was a lot of hysteria in the media about the health risks associated with British beef, and so there was pressure upon Donald to lead a campaign to promote the industry and counteract the adverse publicity that it was facing. For Donald and his marketing team, the timing had to be right, and his message was, '*Advertising too early would be wasteful; we have to be patient until the media noise level comes down.*'

Donald and Gwyn would often hold roadshows when they invited local farmers and their wives to explain their marketing strategy. At one meeting they faced the criticism that they were never on television defending the industry. Gwyn retorted, '*I did twenty-seven radio interviews one Thursday morning, followed by interviews on Sky Television and other television channels.*' Donald then added, '*What*

Gwyn didn't tell you was that he hadn't done Radio One. I've actually done Radio One![33]

When he was sure that the time was right, Donald would put across a marketing message that was simple in its essence: *'Our beef is the safest in the world. Nobody else has taken such comprehensive measures to keep their meat safe.'* Quality assurance standards were promoted to show consumers that measures had been taken to ensure that their meat was safe to eat. In the same speech at the Royal Highland Show where he outlined the catastrophic decline in mince sales, Donald launched the quality minced beef standard with a promotion involving stickers, posters and press and television advertising:

Consumers can buy with confidence all minced beef bearing the standard knowing that it is offal-free, is 100 per cent beef, comes from regular cuts and their trimmings, and is from cattle under thirty months of age. All butchers who wish to carry the standard will have to sign up and certify that their mince conforms to the new standard. Our regional executives will check on twelve hundred butchers each month representing more than ten per cent of all butchers.[34]

As a result, monthly beef sales rose by over fifty per cent in the following six months.

The European Union started to lift the ban on British beef exports in 1999, and this was a time of great jubilation for

---

33. Radio One is the BBC's pop music radio channel, and would not normally be associated with the problems facing the livestock industry.
34. 'MLC pushes mince with new standard' (*Farmers' Weekly*, 28th June 1996).

Donald and the meat industry.[35] At a celebration lunch held in Brussels, hosted by Donald, he said:

This is a very important day for the British beef industry. We have worked long and hard during the past three years to get this ban lifted and now we plan to work even longer and harder to re-establish export markets across the world. Confidence in British beef has already fully returned in Britain – I am confident our message of high safety standards will convince customers across the globe that British beef is a top-quality food.[36]

European consumers had always enjoyed the quality of British beef, so it was imperative that confidence in the safety of British beef was restored. Donald and his colleagues, along with government ministers, appeared at trade fairs to demonstrate the high quality of British beef. Top-quality British chefs were brought along to give practical demonstrations and provide beef samples to the delegates attending the fairs.

The MLC used public relations companies to obtain professional advice on regaining European market confidence. Elizabeth Buchanan, who worked for Bell Pottinger, one of the PR companies used, later went to work for HRH Prince Charles as his Assistant Private Secretary. She provided the link to get the Prince involved in providing practical support in restoring confidence in British beef. He had always been very interested in the

---

35. It did, however, take until 2006 before the ban was completely removed, as a result of some countries, notably France and Germany, refusing to lift the ban, leading to trade disputes and court cases within the EU.
36. 'British beef back in Europe' (*MLC Industry News*, Autumn 1999).

farming industry, and had deep sympathy for the farming community suffering from the impact of BSE on their livelihoods. He agreed to be involved in a plan to work with European chefs to let them taste again the excellence of British beef. The MLC, under Donald, hosted meetings in France and Italy with influential leaders and chefs. Prince Charles and Donald hosted a three-day visit of top chefs from all over Europe, which included visits to farms and abattoirs, ending up at Highgrove House where they were fed some beef from the Prince's estate. The involvement of Prince Charles in the European marketing strategy played a hugely significant part in boosting beef exports. Donald explained, '*Without the support of His Royal Highness, it would have taken much, much longer, and his help was crucial in persuading Europeans to accept our beef again.*' The Prince and Donald remained friends after this and worked together on other projects.

There was one other major plague on livestock during Donald's time as MLC Chair. That was, of course, the foot-and-mouth outbreak in 2001, which we mentioned in chapter two. In that chapter we described how the disease spread quickly from the first diagnosed pig from Heddon-on-the-Wall in Northumberland to farms throughout the country. Donald and Ben Gill, NFU President, had regular meetings with Nick Brown, the Agriculture Minister. They worked together to persuade the government (often against the advice of government officials) to stop the movement of livestock and to implement a policy of slaughtering infected animals and those animals on neighbouring farms.

There was a major debate as to whether livestock should be slaughtered or whether a vaccination programme should be introduced. Although Donald overall supported slaughter as the correct policy, he did regret that they did not trial a vaccination programme in a small controlled area, so that they could learn lessons for the future.

By the end of 2001 the disease was under control, but that came at the cost of slaughtering six million animals. As a farmer, Donald had himself lost two hundred cattle.

The End of Donald's Chairmanship

Although BSE was the major issue affecting Donald's time as MLC Chair and the one that most brought him to the attention of the general public (including Radio One listeners!), he had a number of other issues that he had to deal with.

Another health scare, similar to the alleged link between BSE and vCJD, was the supposed link between red meat consumption and colon cancer. In 1997 the Committee on Medical Aspects of Food and Nutrition Policy (COMA) reported that such a link existed and that consumers should reduce their red meat consumption. Shortly after COMA reported, Donald was keynote speaker at the British Veterinary Association Congress in Edinburgh. He deviated from his prepared address to refute these claims. He said:

> *It simply isn't true that science supports the case for a link between red meat and colon cancer. In the balance against COMA's work, you have to put eight significant and recent studies carried out across Europe, none*

of which finds any evidence of a connection between eating red meat and colon cancer. Indeed, there appears to be no difference in colon cancer rates between meat eaters and vegetarians. A common-sense look at the statistics seems to support this view. Red meat consumption has fallen by twenty-five per cent over the past twenty years, yet the incidence of colon cancer has increased by twenty per cent over the same period.

We accept that people who eat a lot of red meat, without balancing that sensibly with fruit and vegetables, ought to look at their diet. But what we cannot accept is that these recommendations might frighten people who should be eating more red meat into eating less when there is no valid scientific basis for it.

In his position, Donald was prepared to use reasoned argument to protect the industry. He did, however, sometimes receive criticism that he was neglecting particular sectors of the industry. Pig breeders were a case in point. The pig sector is very cyclical (what Americans term 'the hog cycle'); when the market is doing well, breeders flood the market, and then the price drops, leading to a scaling back in supply. This cycle makes it very hard to stabilise the market and plan effectively. The pig sector felt that Donald and the MLC were not giving them enough support, particularly in their competition with chicken. They wanted greater independence and more support. Donald agreed that pig farmers were going through an exceptionally difficult period. Writing in the summer 1998 edition of *MLC Industry News* he said:

The pig industry is in crisis. Producers are accustomed to the cyclical nature of pig farming but this is, for many, the most serious crisis in their business experience.

The Commission agreed to their request and gave them greater independence with a dedicated team to support them, along with a financial injection to help them with their marketing.

Another area where Donald had to use his negotiating skills was in relation to Scottish and Welsh devolution. When Labour, under Tony Blair, came into power in 1997, they pledged to provide Scotland and Wales with devolved governments. The expectation that Scottish and Welsh farmers had was that the powers of the MLC should also be devolved to the respective nations, particularly over how the levies raised by the MLC should be spent in Scotland and Wales. Donald came up with a solution that he believed would be accepted by all parties involved. Certain responsibilities, such as economic analysis, generic marketing and product development, would be retained centrally by the MLC on a Great Britain basis, whereas the use of levies for marketing, promotion and research would be delegated to the nations. When Donald explained his plan to (now Sir) Richard Packer, the MAFF Permanent Secretary, his response was, *'Don't agree a plan that requires angels to make it work or that depends on your personal relationships!'* Sir Richard was absolutely right, because the plan fell apart after Donald had left office.

As MLC Chair, Donald was occasionally asked to use his influence in related organisations. One of these organisations was Food from Britain, which was chaired by his predecessor at MLC, Geoffrey John. As its name suggests, Food from Britain was established to promote British food exports, and of course because meat exports were so important within the overall food export market, Donald was asked to join its council in 1994. He played a key role by attending trade fairs in different European cities, and got to know well the food attaches attached to the different embassies.

He also became very friendly with his colleagues on the council of Food from Britain who were, in the main, chief executives of food processors. One such colleague was Sir James Walker, the leading family member of Walker's Shortbread, based in the village of Aberlour in Speyside, Scotland. On one occasion when Donald and Rhoda were on holiday in Speyside with Donald's cousin John Murray and his wife Rosalind, they visited Aberlour. They were walking down the street when a Range Rover drove past and then suddenly put its brakes on. James Walker jumped out of the car and exclaimed, '*Don Curry! What are you doing in Aberlour?*' Donald explained that they were here for a weekend, and so James invited them for coffee. They went back to his house and James made them coffee. As he poured it, this great biscuit magnate embarrassingly had to confess, '*You'll never believe this, but I can't find a biscuit in the house!*'

Donald retired from his position as MLC Chair in 2001, having had his term of office extended by one year, as MAFF had not got round to finding a replacement. The extra year gave Donald the opportunity to finish off work on BSE, as well as leading the Commission at the beginning of the foot-and-mouth crisis.

Donald enjoyed working with the team that he had around him, some of whom had very appropriate names. In a letter to *The Spectator* in a response to an article on nominative determinism, whereby your name may have an influence on your occupational choice, Adrian Bell recalled:

> *In the early 2000s MLC employed a marketing manager called Chris Lamb. David Trotter was responsible for sales development, the pig meat product manager was Mo Herd, and it was all overseen by chairman Don Curry (now Lord Curry of Kirkharle). Then there was the press officer, John Bullock.*[37]

Donald was highly regarded in his role by all who worked with him, whether they were fellow commissioners, directors, staff, politicians, civil servants or members of the farming community. As we have already mentioned, he was seen as a man of integrity who could be trusted, and who had the best interests of farmers, processors, retailers and consumers at heart. People knew of his Christian faith, and this added to the trust that people placed in him.

Because of his Christian humility he did not seek formal recognition of his services, but he received it nonetheless with two visits to Buckingham Palace to receive honours from Her Majesty the Queen. In 1997 he received the honour of Commander of the Order of the British Empire for his work in dealing with the BSE crisis. This was a major event in Donald's life, although his mother, Barbara,

---

37. Adrian Bell, 'Name Games' (*The Spectator*, 1st March 2025).

whom he took as a guest, did complain about not getting a cup of tea. The second occasion was in 2001 when he received a knighthood, and it was his friend Prince Charles who carried out the official duty that day. That was a fitting tribute to his selfless service at the MLC.

CHAPTER SIX

The Curry Commission

Giving the Prime Minister a Holiday Boost

If Donald was expecting a peaceful life away from the hubbub of government policy-making and agricultural politics after he stepped down from the MLC, he was in for a shock. In August 2001, five months after retiring from his role as MLC Chair, Donald was working on a digger, trying to unblock drains in one of his fields that had serious drainage problems, when his mobile phone rang. It was Downing Street.

Agriculture was a major concern for Prime Minister Tony Blair and his officials. The meat crises of the '90s were still fresh in people's minds, and foot-and-mouth disease was still leading to the large-scale slaughter of animals, although it was now, by the second half of 2001, being brought under control. In addition, the European Union's Common Agricultural Policy was continuing to produce huge mountains of surplus grain. Members of the public saw this as an immoral waste of food in a world where millions of people faced a daily battle to obtain enough food to feed their families and fend off starvation. There was also a growing concern that the overproduction of grain and the intensive production of livestock were damaging the environment. It seemed that farming incentives were working in a perverse way to produce more and more food that was simply not required within Europe while simultaneously causing great harm to the environment. Downing Street believed that there had to be a major review of agricultural policy – and that Donald was the man to lead it.

Donald, however, was possibly not Downing Street's first choice. When he received the phone call that August, Donald was asked by the senior official who called him if he would consider chairing a policy commission looking into the future of agriculture. Donald's response was, '*Chairing it? I had heard a rumour that I might be asked to join the Commission, but I never for a moment thought that I would be considered for the Chair.*' The official reassured him that he was definitely being asked to chair the Commission. Donald's reply was, '*So have other people refused then?*', knowing full well that at least one other person had turned the offer down. The official gave a hesitant, stuttering reply, '*No, no, you were always on our list, you were always on our list.*' Donald said that he would have to think about it and talk it over with his wife as it was a large, responsible undertaking. The official asked him how long he would need. Donald asked him, '*Why, is there some urgency?*' '*Well*', he replied, '*we would like to make an announcement tomorrow.*' Donald, with his northern humour, replied, '*Well, you've been leaving it to the last minute. You can't tell me that I am first on your list if you are leaving it this late to give me an invitation.'* Donald agreed to phone him the following day with his response.

Donald and Rhoda discussed it that evening and, as they always did over such decisions, they prayed about it to be sure that they were doing what God wanted them to do. Donald decided to take on the role. He knew that it was an important job that had to be done and his experience with the MLC, and not least as a hands-on farmer, would stand him in good stead. The following morning Donald phoned the official and said that he agreed to take on the role. The official said, *'The Prime Minister will be pleased that you have agreed to take this on.'* Donald had read two days earlier that Tony Blair had taken his family on holiday to Mexico, and so did not really believe that the appointment of Chair would be very high on his holiday agenda. Nevertheless, he said to the official, *'You had better ring him up then, and tell him to relax and enjoy his holiday, knowing that I have agreed to do this.'*

Donald met Tony Blair in person early the following month. He insisted on the Prime Minister intervening personally if he did not get cooperation from officials, saying, *'If I have problems with engagement, I need to knock on your door.'* In fact Donald had to contact Downing Street twice on different issues, and the Prime Minister was as good as his word, giving Donald the support that he needed.

The Commission at Work

The Policy Commission on the Future of Farming and Food was set up with appointments made in August 2001.

It was a very distinguished body of ten men and women who were all highly capable professionals coming from a diverse range of fields, and all having much to offer in terms of expertise and experience. One member of the Commission, DeAnne Julius, a formidable Anglo-American economist who was one of the founding members of the Bank of England's Monetary Policy Committee, was brought in to ensure that the recommendations made by the Commission were affordable and would produce the desired economic outcomes. The Commission had a secretariat from the Department for Environment, Food and Rural Affairs (DEFRA)[38] working for them, led by a high-flying civil servant, James Quinault, whom Donald remembers particularly as an avid daily reader of both *The Guardian* and *Le Monde*.

The remit that the Commission was given was to:

Advise the Government on how we can create a sustainable, competitive and diverse farming and food sector which contributes to a thriving and sustainable rural economy, advances environmental, economic, health and animal welfare goals, and is consistent with the Government's aims for Common Agriculture Policy (CAP) reform, enlargement of the EU and increased trade liberalisation.[39]

This was undoubtedly a huge remit to fulfil. What made it even more difficult was that the final report was expected

---

38. DEFRA was created in June 2001, replacing the former Ministry of Agriculture, Fisheries and Food, but also taking responsibility for environmental protection, wildlife and the countryside.
39. Policy Commission on the Future of Farming and Food, *Farming and Food: a Sustainable Future* (2002), p. 5.

to be completed and published by the end of the year. The Commission managed to negotiate an additional month, and so the final publication date was extended to January 2002.

The group had the first of its almost weekly meetings on 6th September. During their meetings they had intense conversations on the evidence presented to them, reflecting on what they had heard and considering how the industry could be transformed. Donald began by encouraging the group to formulate a vision as to where they would like the industry to be in twenty years' time, and, from there, to analyse the current state of food and farming and how the gap might be closed. He hoped that in this way the group would be able to put forward proposals that would create the outcomes that would meet the requirements of their remit.

One member of the Commission, Iain Ferguson, who at the time was CEO of Birds Eye Wall's, summarised his view of the state of the industry as follows:

We had a food industry that had become broadly disconnected from its production base, or to look at it the other way, a production base that had become disconnected from its customers. It was the move from local production, local consumption to specialised production and consumption based through major manufacturers, which was a very different shape of supply chain, with people no longer eating what was produced on their doorstep. With transport and logistics, they are able to eat what is produced all over the country and indeed all over the world. The source of the food when you looked at consumer research was seen as the retailer or the restaurant, and no longer the farm or the food company.

The members of the Commission were all highly successful, intelligent men and women who had their own views on how to move the industry forward. Potentially there was much scope for disagreement, and Donald would have to make use of the diplomatic skills that he had deployed so successfully at the MLC. He laid down the ground rules right from the start:

This is how this is going to be managed. We are going to share everything. We are going to work through whatever disagreements we might have around the table, and we shall sit until the middle of the night if we have to, to reach agreement. What I am not having is somebody writing a supplementary report because they disagreed with what was in the main one. When we have finished this, we are all going to sign up to whatever it is that we have agreed, and we are going to be united. Furthermore, we are all going to ensure that whatever we recommend is as far as possible delivered, and so we are not going to draft recommendations that have not a chance of being approved. We are going to draft recommendations that government will find acceptable, but which will also demonstrably change behaviour. And I also hope that it will be a fun experience.

This was tough talking on Donald's part, and there was also tough action. He can remember on two occasions sending Commissioners who strongly disagreed with each other on a policy recommendation to sit in a room, and they were told not to come out until they found agreement. Donald's approach seemed to work. One of the Commissioners, (now Dame) Fiona Reynolds, at the time Director General of the National Trust, spoke very highly of Donald's chairing of the meetings:

Don was a bit of an unknown quantity. We had no idea what he would be like as the Chair, but to his enormous credit he encouraged us to think radically and differently and to be really ambitious for a new future, which, for sure, there needed to be for farming and food. He was very good at drawing consensus from a disparate group of people.

Iain Ferguson described Donald as having *'a hugely authentic and an incredibly genuine approach to life that gets people around him, because they* want *to be around him, as he is very generous with his time and his interest'.*

The group formed a very strong bond and worked together to produce a series of recommendations, one hundred and four in all, that, apart from four, were accepted by government. This bond remained well after the report was published, and indeed in 2023, more than twenty years after the publication of the report, eight of the Commissioners met as Donald's guests for lunch in the House of Lords.

Before making recommendations, of course, they had to undertake research into the current state of agriculture. They issued a written call for evidence and received about thirteen hundred responses from a wide range of farming, manufacturing and retailing bodies, as well as councils and other public bodies. Over three hundred individuals also responded with their personal views. They also met with fifty-five different interest groups and organisations. The Commission members as a group had to sift through this evidence and reflect on what they had read and heard. Although they all had their areas of expertise, they felt it was important that they examined the evidence in a holistic way so that they could all see the bigger picture.

They also went on five regional visits, including a visit to St James's Palace to meet Prince Charles. Deirdre Hutton (now Dame and at the time Chair of the National Consumer Council) recalls that particular visit on 6th December:

The room was incredibly dark because it was a large room and all round the room there were these light-saving bulbs, and as a consequence you could hardly see anybody. Prince Charles turned to me and asked whether I didn't agree that there was too much regulation on farmers and that it would be much better if most of it were abolished and farmers were just left to produce food as they had done for generations. He was expecting me to say yes in agreement, but I had to say no. Farmers had to understand that they were part of the food chain and that regulation was there to protect consumers from ill health. This was an answer that went down very badly.

Donald also had to discuss the emerging findings with EU officials, and in particular with the Agricultural Commissioner, Franz Fischler. One of the proposals was to decouple support for farmers from the level of production, which was counter to existing EU policy, and so was very controversial. There was for Donald a very sad episode during these discussions in Brussels, when on 9th December 2001, while waiting to meet the Commissioner, he received a phone call from his brother Chris to say that their beloved mother Barbara had died. She had been at a service at Armstrong Hall on the Sunday evening and then, after being out for supper with some of her friends, she drove home in the dark. She got out of the car, opened the door but left the key outside still in the lock. She sat down in her chair and quietly passed away.

Neighbours had realised that there was something wrong and phoned Chris who then phoned Donald. Donald decided just to go ahead with the meeting as planned without telling the Commissioner, because if he had told him, *'it would have been too emotional'*. For Donald, his mother's death was very sad, but he had peace because he knew that Barbara was now with her Lord in a better place. After the meeting, Donald immediately flew back to Newcastle. In the end, the EU Agricultural Commission agreed with the proposals that Donald and his colleagues put forward, which resulted in a massive shift in European agricultural policy.

A draft report was produced in December 2001, which Donald took away to do a final proofread and edit. In his own rather unconventional way, he took it with him on a cruise up the Norwegian coast. It gets dark very early there at that time of year, and so Donald had plenty of opportunity to go through the report with a fine-tooth comb. Rhoda whiled away the hours reading as Donald was working.

The Curry Report

The report was published on time in January 2002. Its official title was *Farming and Food: A Sustainable Future*, but people just seemed to refer to it as the Curry Report.

The main theme running through the report was reconnection, to try to overcome the disconnection that Iain Ferguson alluded to above. In the foreword to the report, the Commissioners stated this very clearly:

> *Our central theme is reconnection. We believe the real reason why the present situation is so dysfunctional is that farming has become detached from the rest of the economy and the environment. The key objective of public policy should be to reconnect our food and farming industry: to reconnect farming with its market and the rest of the food chain; to reconnect the food chain and the countryside; and to reconnect consumers with what they eat and how it is produced.*[40]

As we saw above, Donald encouraged the group to share their vision for farming and food, and their joint vision was incorporated in the first chapter of the report. They wanted agriculture to be profitable and diverse, but also to take its environmental responsibilities seriously through farmers who have *'embraced the management of the land for environmental public good as a key part of what farming is about'.*[41] They visualised a world-class processing industry and saw retailing and catering to be important components of the supply chain. Local food economies should be

---

40. *Farming and Food: A Sustainable Future* (2002), p. 6.
41. *Farming and Food: A Sustainable Future* (2002), p. 9.

developed so that consumers can buy food from their own region. Consumers were to be provided with clear information about the food on offer to them, including what was necessary for healthy eating. They still looked to government to support the industry but not to control it, particularly as they were coming to the time when the European Union's Common Agricultural Policy was to be renegotiated.

The timing of the report was just right, and one can see why Downing Street wanted to get the Commission together so quickly and then to push them on to meet a very tight deadline. As the report stated:

Farming, like many manufacturing and production industries, has had its worst years during a time of prosperity for the country as a whole.[42]

There were a number of reasons for the difficulties faced by farmers. The strength of sterling meant that subsidy payments from the EU were lower in value when exchanged into sterling, and imports from Europe were more competitive than British produce. Agricultural exports were correspondingly relatively more expensive. To make things even more difficult, world food prices had declined, bringing in less income for producers. Farmers also felt squeezed between the growing power of their equipment and chemicals suppliers on the one hand, and the retail giants who can force down the prices paid to farmers on the other. Then, of course, there were the meat

---

42. *Farming and Food: A Sustainable Future* (2002), p. 14.

and livestock crises that had devastated the industry over the previous decade.

Subsidies given to farmers were seen by the Commission as a hindrance to developing the industry to meet consumer demand:

The production subsidies paid to farmers under the CAP have become part of the problem rather than the solution. They divide producers from their market, distort price signals, and mask inefficiency.[43]

The overproduction of grain and the overbreeding of livestock were a direct consequence of the subsidy system that encouraged farmers to produce too much. The solution that the Commission recommended was to decouple subsidies from production, and instead provide support to farmers for enhancing the rural environment, to overcome the loss of hedgerows, the decline of wildlife, and the pollution caused by intensive farming. Farmers were to be encouraged to produce an environmental audit and a whole farm environmental management plan, for which they would receive a one-off payment.

The Commission emphasised that government support was required to meet the public demand for a sustainable rural environment so that the general public could enjoy the pleasures of the countryside:

If society wants environmental benefits (and we believe it does) which cannot be delivered by the market on its

---

43. *Farming and Food: A Sustainable Future* (2002), p. 20.

own then farmers should be rewarded from the public purse for providing them.[44]

They looked to the government to increase what was called 'modulation', diverting a proportion of the production subsidies given to farmers into payments for introducing environmental schemes.

The report recommended that farmers should be encouraged to seek new business opportunities and diversify into other areas, such as hospitality and retailing. They also needed to access new technology to improve productivity and the Commission recommended that the government set up a 'priorities board' for strategic support that would support the farmers. Those farmers who managed small landholdings were encouraged to collaborate with others to share labour and equipment and use their increased negotiating power in the market and in accessing specialist advice. The report also sought to establish a Food Chain Centre, bringing together representatives from each link in the food chain for joint analysis, research and training and collaborative trading relationships.

The Commission also looked to measures that would improve animal health, given the livestock crises that the industry had faced. Using very strong words, they stated:

In view of England's abysmal animal health record in recent years, DEFRA in consultation with the industry need to devise and implement a comprehensive animal health strategy.[45]

---

44. *Farming and Food: A Sustainable Future* (2002), p. 73.
45. *Farming and Food: A Sustainable Future* (2002), p. 50.

The industry needed to regain public confidence, not only in terms of food safety, but also through clear information about the food on offer so that consumers can make rational choices about the food they wished to buy, including buying more local food. Healthy eating was to be encouraged to fight the battle against obesity.

The Commission recognised that there had to be a change in farming's image, as too often the industry was seen as a low-skill, 'dirty' industry providing little economic incentive for younger people to enter the industry:

> *What can change farming's image? A resurgence of the industry, with farm businesses returning to profit and agriculture being seen as a place where innovation is valued. Crucial to that will be regaining a reputation for committed countryside management. We hope that the recommendations in this report will encourage that.*[46]

During the final drafting of the report, Donald met with Treasury officials to cost out the proposals. The Financial Secretary to the Treasury was a fine Christian MP, Paul Boateng, who was in 2002 to become the first UK black Cabinet minister. He was a kind, warm-hearted man who actually sent Rhoda flowers when she was in hospital. It was his job to ensure that the recommendations in the report provided good value for money. The report was accepted by the government at a cost of £500 million.

The report was officially launched to the media on 29th January 2002. The launch was led by Margaret Beckett, the

---

46. *Farming and Food: A Sustainable Future* (2002), pp. 58-59.

Secretary of State for Environment, Food and Rural Affairs, with Donald playing a key role in answering questions.

The media, by and large, seemed to be fairly positive about the report. *The Guardian* in its leader article said this:

> *It is almost too good to be true. The government appointed a commission in August to look into sustainable farming. It started work in September and delivered its final report this month after receiving more than 1,000 submissions. What is more, the recommendations were consensual, even though the commissioners included lobbyists and representatives of supermarkets and the food manufacturing industry. It contains dozens of eminently practical solutions that ten years ago would have been regarded as radical . . . The model of having a fast-track expert commission, including dissenting lobbies, should be extended to new areas in an attempt to solve other problems facing the country where politicians have lost their way . . . And who should chair them? The government could do worse than ring up Sir Donald and ask him what his diary is like.*[47]

Farmers, however, were less positive. Donald took part in a BBC *Newsnight* discussion with his old friend Ben Gill, President of the NFU, chaired by presenter Jeremy Paxman. Ben's view was that the environmental lobby, who were always attacking farmers, had won the argument and that Donald had been seduced by them. He claimed that farmers could not afford to have cash taken away

---

47. 'Quick, right and radical' (*The Guardian,* 30th January 2002), p. 21.

from them. Donald, however, emphasised his view that he wanted a prosperous agricultural sector that also looked after the rural environment. Over the next couple of months Ben mellowed in his views, and at a meeting chaired by the Prime Minister, he introduced his statement by saying:

We fully agree with much of the analysis and many of the conclusions of the report. I would like to make that clear because much of the media focus at the time of the launch was on the few areas where we had important reservations, rather than on the much bigger area of common ground.[48]

Donald took the argument around the country to farmers' meetings, where on occasion there was hostility on the part of farmers. Sometimes this hostility existed because they had not actually read the report. At one meeting where Donald suspected this, he asked his interrogator what he thought about the reference to Madonna contained in the report.[49] The poor man looked baffled, a sure sign that he had not read the report. Some farmers were still looking for DEFRA to solve their problems, but Donald had to point out that while the government would provide support, it was up to farmers to act as businessmen and take new opportunities to deal with arising issues.

The 'Honorary Minister'

On 12th December 2002, the government had produced its strategy document in response to the Commission's report

---

48. Statement by Ben Gill President of the NFU, 26th March 2002.
49. *Farming and Food: A Sustainable Future* (2002), p. 96.

and, as we noted above, accepted one hundred of the Commission's recommendations (only turning down four of them). Their report, entitled *The Strategy for Sustainable Food and Farming: Facing the Future,* outlined what the Government intended to do to take the Commission's recommendations forward. Donald was asked by a Treasury minister if he thought that DEFRA would have the confidence of farmers to take the report forward and deliver its recommendations. In response, Donald had to say honestly that he did not think DEFRA had the trust of farmers to do the job properly. He was then out of the blue asked if he would oversee the process by chairing the implementation group for the strategy.

This was most unusual, as the person who produced a report is very rarely asked to go into government and implement it. Dame Fiona Reynolds put it well:

Normally, these sorts of exercises end with the report being submitted, but this one didn't because Don was given an almost honorary ministerial role to go into DEFRA to implement it, which was an interesting and unusual process for a policy commission.

Although Donald was not officially a minister, he had nevertheless all the trappings of ministerial office. He chaired the implementation with civil servants who answered to him, he had an office in Whitehall, and he worked closely alongside government ministers. He established eight workstreams, each covering a different aspect of the report's recommendations, with the aim of spearheading the delivery of the strategy. As part of its regional policy, the Blair government had established

Regional Development Agencies in each of the English regions, and Donald set up a group in each region to be accountable for the implementation of the strategy. He regularly visited Downing Street to report on progress, and reflecting later he said:

To go in and out of that famous Number 10 door on a reasonably regular basis was an unbelievable experience.

During his time overseeing the implementation of the strategy from 2002 to 2009, Donald visited each of the regions twice a year to monitor the progress being made. On each visit, he convened a meeting of the key stakeholders, where he ensured that he asked probing questions to find out what was happening on the ground, challenging them to share both what was going well and what was not going quite so well. By so doing, he could obtain a reasonably accurate understanding of the changes that were being made. He was also taken to see projects that were examples of best practice, and which he was able to share with other regions. These visits were appreciated by the stakeholders who seemed reassured that they were receiving the right level of support to drive the process forward.

Overall, the groups that he talked to felt positive about the progress the industry was making. For example, he spoke to local food groups and they were pleased with the way that local markets were being developed, so that more food was remaining in the area where it was produced. Progress was also made with environmental issues. By the time that Donald stood down from his role in 2009, a massive seventy per cent of farmland was under environmental management, compared with less than ten per cent when the report was published.

Not everything went smoothly, however. The banking crisis of 2007 and 2008 resulted in a downturn in the economy and did affect progress in the agricultural sector. In addition, the workstream on healthy eating that aimed to deal with issues such as diet and obesity did not make the progress that it should have done, largely due to a degree of internecine rivalry between DEFRA and the Department of Health.

In undertaking his major responsibilities on both the Policy Commission and the Implementation Group, Donald acknowledged that he was working under the hand of God. He wrote an article in the Arthur Rank Centre's publication *Country Way*, including the following final paragraph:

> *God created a perfect world. A world that was sustainable in the fullest sense of the word. Man failed of course, and our stewardship of His creation has not always been as sensitive as it should have been. It continues to challenge us but He is the Sustainer of Life. God provides the spiritual and physical solutions – we do of course have to acknowledge his authority.*[50]

Twenty Years On: The Need for a New Policy Commission?

Much of Europe was affected by farmers' protests in the early weeks of 2024. Convoys of tractors blocked many of the main arteries into cities and roads in city centres.

---

50. Donald Curry, 'Digging for Victory' (*Country Way*, Spring 2004), p. 5.

Barricades were set up, farmers held demonstrations and manure was illegally dumped in front of government offices. They were complaining that they faced competition from cheap imports, and that neither their own government nor the European Union was doing much to support them.

Although the UK is no longer a member of the EU, farmers here had the same grievances against our government, and felt ignored by government ministers and officials. They took to the roads and city centres in their tractors in protest, with London and Kent being the main centres of protest, displaying banners with messages such as '*Save British Farming*' and '*No Farmers, No Food, No Future*'. It does seem that farming is in crisis once again.

Donald shared his thoughts on the current state of farming and the difficult situation that farmers face in a podcast hosted by Liberal Democrat Member of Parliament, Tim Farron, who is himself a Christian politician.[51] He started off the broadcast not talking about farming, but about how amazed he was at the ways in which God has influenced his life over the years, giving him opportunities and responsibilities. He shared his joy at the marriage of his granddaughter, a lovely Christian girl, to a young Christian doctor, and seeing how enthusiastic they are in their faith and how they are living in the joy of the Lord.

Both Donald and Tim were at the NFU conference held in February 2024, and Donald related what he felt was a rather downbeat mood at the conference:

---

51.   *A Mucky Business with Tim Farron* (27th February 2024).

Farmers are going through a period of real uncertainty. There is a deep concern about the future. Everyone accepts that we have left the European Union and we are going through this seven-year transition from the basic payments scheme that farmers were very familiar with . . . That is being dismantled and it is being replaced by new environmental schemes where farmers are paid for public goods. Those public goods are mostly in the environmental box together with public access. There is no way that the support farmers enjoyed under the basic payments scheme is going to be replaced by these environmental payments . . . Farmers are feeling really concerned about the impact of this on their livelihoods.

He recalled that in the past farmers were rewarded for producing food, but then they were not encouraged to consider sufficiently the environmental impact of their activity. With the change in payments systems, a greater emphasis was placed on environmental concerns, but perhaps the pendulum had swung too far the other way away from rewarding farmers for producing food.

The challenge is getting the balance right, the right level of reward for both delivering on the environment and producing food.

He continued by saying that farmers are also concerned about the power of the large supermarkets, as well as the trade deals that have been made that allow imported food to enter the country at lower prices but without the level of regulation that UK farmers face. There is, of course, the real danger of food supplies being disrupted by world events, and so as a nation we may not always be able to rely on our food needs being met from abroad, and so we shall need to have a strong domestic agricultural base.

Discussion moved on to suicides among farmers. The increasing uncertainty of working as a farmer has, in Donald's view, resulted in an increase in the suicide rate within the farming community. He spoke of the tragedy of a young farmer that he knew who had taken his own life and the impact on not just his own family but on the whole local community. Whereas in the past there was more collaboration between farmers, there is now greater isolation and farmers feel more vulnerable. Farming charities such as the Farming Community Network do try to intervene where they believe that someone is vulnerable, but the difficulty is in reaching people in time. Donald sees an increasing role for churches to reach out to those who feel that life has become so dark they have no alternative but to end it.

This podcast discussion demonstrated clearly that agriculture faces mounting problems.

As we have seen, the Curry Report was on the whole well received and heralded a time of promising change for the industry, but now other events such as Brexit, economic downturns and global conflict made life in 2024 much more difficult for farmers. Donald himself has refined his view about what aspects of agriculture should be regarded as public goods; given increased world conflict, food security should now be considered as a public good, and so he feels that there should be support from the taxpayer to help farmers produce enough food for the nation in an increasingly insecure world.

Perhaps it is time for a fresh look at agriculture in the way that Donald did in 2001. He certainly thinks so, and, as one has come to expect of Donald, he took the initiative in 2024 by bringing together like-minded individuals from different parts of the industry to discuss the main issues, with assistance from the Institute of Grocery Distribution. The group, led by Donald, produced a policy discussion document which they sent to Steve Reed, the Secretary of State for DEFRA in June 2025.

The paper outlined the problems facing the industry and proposed a series of recommendations for governments to implement in order to *'have a nation nourished by a transformed food system with a thriving UK agricultural economy'*. The recommendations included the recognition of food security as a public good; moving towards an aspiration of seventy per cent self-sufficiency; the commitment of all stakeholders to long-term environmental improvement; an improved framework for research, innovation, digital technology and innovation; and providing high-quality professional development and training.

In June 2025 Tim Farron raised a question in the House of Commons with Daniel Zeichner, Minister of State for Food Security and Rural Affairs, as to whether he and the Secretary of State had read Donald's report and whether they agreed that the country needs an urgent plan for food security. The Minister replied that he always read any correspondence that Donald sent him, but this time he disagreed with Donald, as he believed that the country was food secure. He did say, however, that he was prepared to meet with Donald and Tim.[52]

The debate will undoubtedly continue and we need, as Donald mentioned at the end of his podcast with Tim, '*to pray for wisdom and discernment*'.

52. Commons Hansard (UK Parliament, 19th June 2025) https://hansard.parliament. uk/Commons/2025-06-19/debates/6F123E0F-19ED-4CFA-878C-3249A9CBA231/ OralAnswersToQuestions (accessed 27.7.25).

CHAPTER SEVEN

Estate Management

First Dabbles in the Property Market

Donald was called for jury service in August 1993. As is often the case on jury service, a lot of time is spent sitting around for long periods waiting to hear a case. He spent three weeks in Newcastle Law Courts, whiling away the hours until he was finally needed. During that time he browsed through copies of the *Newcastle Journal* that were lying in the room. His eyes were particularly drawn to the property section and the very low price of flats that were for sale, and he felt that they might be a good investment.

Buying property was all very new to Donald as, being a tenant farmer, he did not own the property he lived in or the farm that he managed. This meant that he, like so many other tenant farmers, had no property available for his retirement. He decided to take the matter forward and phoned his bank manager to start the process of securing a loan with a view to buying some flats. Finance was agreed, and viewings were arranged before and after his daily sessions in the law courts. Donald described the experience of his three weeks on jury service as *'seeing three trials: being Chair of the jury, increasing his indebtedness by £126,000, and buying six properties in a "dodgy" part of Newcastle (without adequately consulting Rhoda!)'*.

He was now on the property ladder, although he needed to spend a fair bit of money refurbishing and maintaining his properties. It was made more difficult by high crime rates in the area, and they even lost a whole heating system in one flat. He eventually hired a managing agent to deal with difficulties that cropped up. All in all, it was a good investment, with the rental payments received covering the mortgage repayments.

By the time that Donald sold the flats, the property market had substantially risen. The capital appreciation on the flats allowed him to buy an apartment in London in 2004 where he and Rhoda could stay on their many business trips to the city, including as a residence after Donald entered the Lords. They were also able to buy an apartment in Corbridge after they retired from farming in 2018.

Entering the property market enabled Donald to achieve his goal of saving for their retirement. It also gave him some credibility when he applied to become a trustee of certain landed estates. He actually was a real property owner as well as being a tenant farmer! This was to be of particular significance when he applied to be a trustee of the Crown Estate.

The Crown Estate

In 1999 Donald saw an advertisement that interested him, calling for applicants with rural experience to become a non-executive director of the Crown Estate. As its name suggests, the Crown Estate is officially owned by the King, but not since the days of George III has the monarch been at liberty to manage the estate or make any decisions about the estate's assets. Any profit made from the estate is given to the Treasury, who decide the Sovereign Grant to be paid to the King. The estate is an institutional landowner of properties across the country including urban assets such as Regent Street and the St James's area in London, rural assets covering 185,000 acres across England and Wales, and marine assets covering offshore energy, cables and pipelines on the seabed around our coastline.

Donald was invited for interview in the opulent surroundings of the office of the Crown Estate in 16 Carlton House Terrace by the Chair, Sir Denys Henderson and other members of the board. He talked about his experience in agriculture and also in property management (including his student flats in *a "dodgy" part of Newcastle*, a far cry from Regent Street in London). As a result, he was appointed to the board and served from 2000 to 2007. He felt that his appointment was incredible, saying, '*As far as I know, I am the only tenant farmer ever to have been appointed to the board of the Crown Estate.*'

Of the three divisions of the estate – urban, rural and marine – Donald was expected, along with another board member with an agricultural background, his friend Ian Grant, to have particular oversight of the rural division. He visited each rural estate every three years, meeting with the tenant farmers who managed the land and discussing with them the issues they had. At the end of the visit, they held a dinner for the farmers and their wives. This was appreciated by the estate community as it showed that the institutional landowner based faraway in London was concerned about their welfare. Indeed Donald still meets some of the farmers that he met when he was a board member.

Donald was also fascinated by the marine division, which was a new experience for him. There was, for example, a lot of negotiation between the Department of Industry and the Crown Estate over the licensing of offshore wind farms, leading to the first wind farm being licensed when Donald was a board member. This was a historic first, which was to be followed by a rapid multiplication round the coastline over the next twenty years.

Fish farming was another fascination for him, and his visits to fish farms off the coast of Scotland,[53] including Orkney and Shetland, introduced him to this industry. It is a very capital-intensive industry, with high costs to establish and maintain the farms and to feed the fish. As a result, very few of the salmon farms are family owned any longer, but rather they are large corporate ventures, often Scandinavian in origin.

One visit to the fish farmers in Shetland did backfire, as the farmers resented having to pay rent to the Crown Estate. Their argument was that property rights did not extend to the sea, thus making the seabed communally owned and exempt from rental payments. The Shetland fishermen decided to boycott the meeting with Donald and the others representing the Crown Estate, although

53. Since 2017, Crown Estate Scotland manages the estate portfolio for Scotland including fish farming. When Donald was a board member, the Crown Estate looked after its Scottish interests.

they made a slight concession by sending one man to meet with the delegates. This fisherman gave the party a ride in his boat through thick fog. They could hardly see anything in front of them until they came to a large red hopper that was his tank for the feed for his fish. Being red, it stood out like a beacon in the fog, and so Donald asked him why he had painted it red. The man replied, *'Aye, it's red. The planners wanted me to paint it grey, but we don't want everything to be grey. We live in a grey world. Everything has to be grey, and so I painted it red.'* The actions of the fisherman exemplified the rebellious temperament of many of the Shetlanders. *The Shetland Times* did not hesitate to report on how the fish farmers boycotted the meeting with the Crown Estate.

This was reinforced at a dinner in Lerwick that same day for local authority leaders and prominent individuals, one of whom was the harbour master who sat next to Donald. Donald remarked in conversation that he had seen lots of Shetland ponies during their visit, and that he was reminded of the Shetland pony that he had as a boy on the farm. His pony had been, as Donald recalled, awkward and very strong minded. The harbour master replied, *'Sonny, everything is awkward on Shetland! The ponies are awkward, the sheep are awkward and the people, they are really awkward!'*

Donald enjoyed his time on the board of the Crown Estate and learned a lot there, from managing property portfolios to the difficulties faced by Shetland fish farmers.

The Leckford Estate

During his time on the Meat and Livestock Commission and working on the Policy Commission, Donald got to know many of the chief executives in the retail trade, often at meetings of the Institute of Grocery Distribution. One of those whom he got to know well was Mark Price, Managing Director of Waitrose, part of the John Lewis Partnership. Mark subsequently asked him if he would be willing to become Chair of the management board of the Leckford Estate. Donald accepted and became Chair in 2007.

Leckford is an estate of about three thousand acres in the heart of Hampshire, with both extensive farmland and land available for the general public to use for leisure pursuits, including fishing in the lakes, playing golf, admiring the water gardens, and visiting the farm shop and café. It was purchased in 1929 by John Spedan Lewis, a visionary businessman (as well as being an agricultural experimenter) who was to become founder of the John Lewis Partnership. As the estate developed it provided food to be sold in the business, as well as holiday facilities that were used by the partners. In 1946 the estate officially became part of the John Lewis Partnership, which meant that staff on the estate became partners, sharing in the partnership's profits. In 2001 the estate became part of the Waitrose division of the partnership and grew produce to be sold in Waitrose shops, becoming known as the Waitrose Farm.

Donald saw the estate as '*an interesting and diverse business*', set in beautiful surroundings. The business was, however, losing money every year, with its income failing to meet its costs, particularly its high overhead costs. There was, for example, a lovely country house that John Spedan Lewis had originally bought as his family home, but which was now used for meetings and strategy days by the Waitrose board; they could retreat from the office and plan strategy in idyllic surroundings. The house and extensive parkland were, however, expensive facilities to maintain and service.

During his period as Chair, Donald led the board in making changes to the running of the estate to increase its profitability. The agricultural business was very diverse with a large dairy herd, cereal and oilseed rape production, the production of chicken, eggs and mushrooms, the growing of apples, pears and other fruit in their orchards, and the production of dairy products in their dairy processing plant. Most of this produce was sent to Waitrose. It was decided to create a Leckford brand identity and concentrate on marketing produce that Waitrose would find difficult to source elsewhere. For example, they developed this new brand identity in mushrooms, producing chestnut brown mushrooms rather than the normal white mushrooms that Waitrose could more cheaply import from large production facilities in Ireland. The board also commissioned its own vineyard in 2009, with Donald being quoted in *The Waitrose Chronicle* saying, '*It's a great opportunity – but we will have to be patient and wait for the results!*'[54]

The board also developed the leisure side of the business, so that families could come and enjoy a good day out together. Trout fishing was heavily promoted, as the River Test that ran through the estate had the reputation of having the best trout fishing in Britain; hundreds of people bought

---

54. 'Putting the fizz into Leckford' (*The Waitrose Chronicle*, 30th May 2009).

licences to fish the lakes and the river. The dredging of a lake was commissioned to restore its use as a fishing lake. Golf and the water gardens were heavily promoted, and a new visitor centre was built, including a farm shop and café adjacent to the garden centre. This was a significant development that took place on Donald's watch, about which he was very enthusiastic.

Donald was required to meet regularly with Sir Charlie Mayfield, the Chair of the John Lewis Partnership, and with the Waitrose board to report on progress with Leckford. He got to know them well and won their respect. By the time he stood down as Chair in 2014, they could all see the changes that had been made and the progress that had been achieved. The estate had made great strides towards a break-even position by the time that Donald left the business.

Leckford was a special place that gave Donald great pleasure as he worked hard to develop its potential and profitability. It was for him a huge privilege to have responsibility for an estate that had John Spedan Lewis's footprint all over it.

The Clinton Devon Estate

Exeter Cathedral was packed out on Monday 15th July 2024, as almost a thousand dignitaries, landowners, other members of the farming community, friends and family from all over Devon and beyond gathered together for a memorial service to celebrate the life of Gerard Fane Trefusis, twenty-second Baron Clinton, who had died at the age of eighty-nine earlier in the year. Donald had been invited to speak at the service by Charles, the new Lord Clinton. In his eulogy he spoke very warmly of the first time that he had met Lord Clinton about forty years before:

This should have been a rather daunting experience for a working farmer from Northumberland, encountering one of the most prominent landowners from the south-west of England, but it wasn't, because Gerard Clinton was so unassuming and easy to talk to.

He was very impressed by Lord Clinton's knowledge of practical farming and farming policy:

Gerard's interest in farming policy and politics never wavered. He read every magazine, lots of newspapers, listened to the farming programme at 5.45 every morning and was incredibly well informed. I found it very embarrassing when having breakfast at Heanton or latterly at Blackberry he would ask what I thought about a particular item on the farming programme that morning – I had to confess I was still fast asleep and had missed it.

Donald spoke about him as a wonderful family man, and also as a role model employer:

It is not a fluke that the Clinton Devon Estate has received numerous awards and has repeatedly been included in the Sunday Times list of 'best small companies to work for'. It is a huge accolade to the estate ethos that was set by Gerard. He loved the Clinton Devon Estate and his employees loved to work for him. He was caring, considerate, respectful and interested in the lives of the people working for the estate. He and Nicky [his wife, Lady Clinton] knew everyone and understood their personal circumstances, visiting and supporting those who needed help. It took him twenty minutes to walk through the office as he stopped by desks to greet and chat.

Donald saw him as a humble man, who followed his family motto:

Yet he did not seek glory or personal recognition. A humble man who was almost embarrassed by the success and attention Clinton Devon Estate has received over the years. In fact, he was a great example of how to live out the family motto, 'Everything comes from God'. This clearly shaped his life. It is a great motto, for it reinforces our dependence on God for everything we do.

Donald had become a trustee of Clinton Devon Estate in 2009. As we mentioned in the introduction to this book, it was in a court case in 2019 alleging corporate manslaughter against the estate that Donald was called as an expert witness, and was described by the barrister for the defence as '*no toff*'. By this time he had developed a great admiration, not only for Lord Clinton, but for the whole operation of the estate, as led by the chief executive, John Varley.

John was appointed to this post in 2000, with no experience at all of estates management, having had senior management roles with British Telecom. Running a barony dating back to 1299, comprising 25,000 acres of land, seems a totally different challenge to helping to lead a worldwide telecommunications company. John, however, does not quite see it that way as he was able to transfer his experience of managing changes in global technology to managing changes in agriculture, especially in the years following Brexit. He sees estate management as '*the land of opportunity*'.

The estate is seen as very forward-looking, a reflection of the vision shared by both the late Lord Clinton and John Varley. Its mission statement is:

> *Doing Today What is Right for Tomorrow:*
> *By handing on the land to future generations in a*
> *better condition;*
> *By protecting habitats, wildlife and natural systems;*
> *By investing in the local community.*[55]

As a trustee, Donald very much bought into that vision, and he saw his role and that of the other trustees in supporting the estate management and the family in bringing that vision to fruition. He wished to ensure the continuity and sustainability of the estate, preserving its unique character and ethos. He was particularly supportive of its innovative approach to protecting the environment, as, for example, in the Lower Otter Valley project that aims to enhance '*the wildlife value of the Lower Otter from local to international significance*'.[56]

Given his experience, Donald was able to contribute much to trustee discussions, especially in relation to the farming business. There were four formal meetings a year, but Donald was called upon for advice at least once

---

55. https://clintondevon.com/ (accessed 13.8.24).
56. https://clintondevon.com/conservation/ (accessed 13.8.24).

a week. John Varley describes the way that he contributed to meetings:

Don brings wise counsel to trustee meetings. He does not speak forcefully, but he speaks powerfully. What he says is based on real world experience. He is completely grounded in everything that he says and does. He has been a good check and balance for some of the more audacious ideas, and while he wouldn't stop progress or push back on innovation, what he would do was either caution a direction of travel or suggest further understanding and analysis before a decision was made.

He has also learned much from being associated with an estate run by an aristocratic family, which is quite different from his own relatively small family business or an institutional landowner, such as the Crown Estate. Donald was greatly respected by the family, and as the late Lord Clinton's daughter, Caroline, said:

Whatever came up, whether it was good or challenging, Don was always there to support or celebrate. He is a great enthusiast with his lovely twinkly smile. He is a very warm person, and he was very good at managing all of the family dynamics.

Donald viewed Clinton Devon as a business with deep roots in the past but which wants to make a significant difference to the welfare of future generations of farmers as well as to the whole of its local community in the present. The high regard with which the estate is held explains why so many people attended Lord Clinton's memorial service.

He stepped down from the board in autumn 2024, having been encouraged by the late Lord Clinton to stay longer than originally planned. Looking back, he is proud to have been associated with such a successful and unique business. He found stepping down quite emotional, having established lasting relationships with the Clinton family, for whom he has enormous respect.

CHAPTER EIGHT

Donald and Science

The Royal Agricultural Society of England

The Royal Agricultural Society of England (RASE) was established in 1838 and received its royal charter from Queen Victoria in 1840. Its aim was to encourage agricultural scientific research and the application of that research into more efficient farming practice. Perhaps it is most noted for running the Royal Show, which was first held in 1839 and continued until 2009, when RASE decided that it could no longer afford to run it. Donald and Rhoda attended the show each year from the mid-1970s until its final demise.

When Donald became Chair of the MLC in 1993, he was also appointed to the Council of RASE. The Society established a sub-committee called Practice with Science (named after the Society's motto) to identify areas of science requiring further research, as well as exploring existing knowledge on particular subjects to communicate to farmers. Donald chaired this committee from 2006 until 2009, and became increasingly fascinated by the role of science in agricultural development. Under his chairmanship, for example, the committee produced a report on the fundamental importance of soil and water management, aspects of farm management that had been largely neglected for many years.[57] It is now generally accepted that effective soil and water management are critical to sustainable farming and food production. Donald's committee's report helped to put this topic on the national farming agenda.

Donald's experience on this committee whetted his appetite to explore further the contribution of scientific research to farming practice.

The Lawes Trust

Donald was a trustee of the Lawes Trust from 2009 to 2017. He was invited on to the trust board by its then Chair, Lord John de Ramsay. He knew Lord de Ramsey well, as he had been President of the Country Land and Business Association, the first Chair of the Environment Agency and a member of the Agricultural Forum.

The trust was established by Sir John Lawes, a nineteenth-century agronomist and a leading developer of the artificial fertiliser industry starting from the fertiliser factory that he set up in 1842. The following year he went on to establish the Rothamstead Experimental Station in Hertfordshire, the oldest agricultural research station in the world. Sir John set up the trust in 1889 to enable the

---

57. Richard Godwin, Gordon Spoor, Brian Finney, Mike Hann and Bryan Davies, *The Current Status of Soil and Water Management in England* (Royal Agricultural Society of England, 2008).

site at Rothamstead to continue its work into crop research. The aim of the trust as summarised on its website is:

> *To advance the science of agriculture for the public benefit through original investigation and research, which may embrace all or any subject(s), connected to or bearing upon agriculture, including animal or vegetable physiology, meteorology, botany and chemistry.*[58]

It continues to be recognised as one of the most important crop and soil research centres in the world, specialising in genetic modification and the gene editing of plants.

Donald thoroughly enjoyed his time on the board of the trust as he was able to be involved in areas that were of great interest to him, such as research priorities, investment in new facilities, the use of buildings and property management. He was also able to be involved in negotiations between government officials and the trust over funding priorities.

Food and Farming Futures

In 2012 Mark Price, Managing Director of Waitrose, and Professor Wayne Powell, Director of the National Institute of Agricultural Botany (NIAB), had conversations that led to the establishment of an organisation that would later be called Food and Farming Futures (F&FF). Mark was concerned about retailers purchasing cheaper produce from abroad rather than obtaining sustainable sourced food from British farms. He wanted to improve communication

---

58.   https://lawestrust.org/ (accessed 17.10.24).

among farmers, processors and retailers, and for them all to share key information and knowledge. In particular, he wanted farmers to have access to the latest scientific knowledge and to apply it in their production processes. This would lower costs and create a more sustainable supply chain.

Wayne invited Donald to chair the body. They formed a board including scientists from various universities and institutions, such as NIAB, the Scottish Agricultural College and Aberystwyth (who provided secretarial and office support), Edinburgh, Newcastle, Queen's Belfast and Harper Adams Universities, that were all carrying out agricultural research. They organised conferences, seminars and workshops that were very popular, bringing together policy makers, scientists and practitioners to share information and explore best practice. The National Library for Agri-Food was set up as a one-stop shop for the latest scientific knowledge and applied research related to agriculture.

Reports on topics related to agricultural science were written by members of F&FF in partnership with university academic experts. One of the most recent was written in 2022 by Donald and Professors Michael Lee and James Lowenberg-DeBoer, both of Harper Adams University, entitled 'Application of Science to Realise the Potential of the Agricultural Transition'.[59] The transition that the authors wanted to see was from Britain having an agricultural sector that lagged behind other advanced countries in terms of productivity and innovation, to

59.   https://farmpep.net/group/727 (accessed 19.10.24).

having an agricultural sector that uses the latest available research to increase efficiency and output.

The basic reason for this relatively low productivity was the fragmented nature of the flow of scientific knowledge from research to the farm. The country was fortunate to have a strong research ethos in agricultural science in a number of its higher-education institutions. The fruits of this research were not, however, reaching our farms in a sufficiently powerful way as to make a significant difference to farming practices. As a result, productivity was not growing in the sector, compared with the experience of other countries that were more effective in applying academic research in practical ways.

This fundamental issue, the authors believed, needed to be dealt with to ensure that the country had a high level of food security where people had access to sufficient, safe and nutritious food. The authors believed that food security is a public good (as is clean air), as one person's sense of food security does not diminish another person's sense of food security. With the fear of global pandemics and a more dangerous geopolitical environment, there was increasing food insecurity, as we saw during the early stages of Covid-19 and the Russian invasion of Ukraine. The issue became more urgent as farming needed to reduce its carbon footprint in line with government carbon net-zero targets. This all means that the government needed to step into the market to ensure that British farmers are producing enough food to meet consumer demand.

Donald and the two professors recommended a number of actions in the report to bring about a radical improvement of British farming productivity. The authors identified the need for government to allocate more funding to the delivery of scientific knowledge. Universities need to strengthen the applied nature of the research that they undertake so that it changes farming practices. Careers advice needed to be given in schools to encourage talented young people to enter the industry to apply new technology. The operation of Agri-Tech Centres that aimed to bring new science and technology to farms should be rationalised. A new 'What Works Centre' should be established to promote agricultural innovation.

The report was released at a breakfast briefing hosted by Donald in the House of Lords in November 2022, attended by farming leaders, scientists, officials from DEFRA and members of the House of Lords. Policy makers are still working through the recommendations outlined in the report, but progress has been made in some areas. For example, the Agri-Tech Centres have merged together into one centre. Daniel Zeichner, a minister in DEFRA, has assured Donald of the department's support in promoting collaboration.

Waitrose provided funding for the organisation's activities for about six years; this funding was invaluable in these early years. The supermarket chain Morrison's also provided support. Funding for F&FF has been more difficult to procure in recent years. The Institute of Agriculture and Horticulture (TIAH), which we shall mention in the next chapter, took over the operation of the National Library for Agri-Food; this greatly reduced the financial burden on F&FF. Donald has also used his network to acquire funding from different sources to keep the organisation being able to provide valuable information for the agricultural sector.

Cawood Scientific

In 2014 Donald received a call from Nigel Patrick, whom he had known previously when Nigel worked for West Cumberland Farmers, an agricultural supply co-operative. Nigel was now a partner in Cawood Scientific, the largest analytical company in the United Kingdom serving the agricultural sector. The core of the business was analysing soil, feed, grain, silage, waste and indeed anything related to the production of livestock and the growing of crops. Customers would contact Cawood for these analytical services, and by 2014 the business's turnover was about £10 million.

Four years earlier, Nigel and his colleague, Linda Radnor, the Operations Manager, had organised a management buyout of the company. Donald's good friend, Sir Ben Gill, former NFU President, had chaired the company since the management buyout. Sadly, Ben died of cancer, and so Nigel and Linda had to find a replacement. Before his death, Ben suggested to them that Donald would be a suitable person to take over the Chair. They set up a shortlist of eminent people. They ended up, however, following Ben's advice and sought to appoint Donald because he, like Ben, had a large network of contacts in agriculture, contacts who would hopefully open doors for them.

They emailed him at the House of Lords, not really expecting a reply, but within a week they received a response and they all agreed to meet. Donald found them to be very persuasive, and he felt that Cawood would be an interesting business to be involved in and a complete contrast to his other roles, as he had never before been involved in a commercial business that was funded by private equity. Nigel and Linda had taken a significant risk when they borrowed money to fund the buyout. Donald himself had to invest to buy shares in the business in order to take on the role of Chair.

The original private equity investor was NVM, but in 2017 they decided to exit the business, and so Donald led the board in searching for another financial partner. After what he called 'a beauty parade' and much negotiation, they settled on a company called Inflection. This, however, was not the end of such negotiations, because the nature of the private equity market meant that growing, successful businesses like Cawood Scientific became targets for acquisition by other private equity companies. This was difficult for Nigel and Linda, as with each change in investor there were subsequent changes in the composition of the board and increased pressure to cut costs. Linda recalled:

> For someone who really cared about the business, to see private equity coming in to strip the business in order to sell it on, that was a real challenge. It was difficult to hold the morals and the values of the company, and the people all still needed looking after, while in the background you had all these accountants just looking at the money. Don was fantastic at looking after us during that whole period of time.

In 2019 they were taken over by a Dutch private equity firm, Waterland. Nigel and Linda decided to step down from day-to-day management, although they remained on the board as non-executive members. Donald led the recruitment process to find their replacements. Simon Parrington and Jez Smith were appointed respectively as Chief Executive Officer and Operations Manager.

Although he found chairing the board to be interesting, he did not always find it easy. As he put it:

The private equity world is quite hard nosed and can be ruthless. This didn't sit well with me and there were times when I had to stand my ground and resist pressure because of my principles and ethical standards. These private equity companies, when they want to sell a company, could present figures that on the face of it could look very attractive, but there is quite a lot of creative accounting that goes on to try to project what they have achieved in the success of investing in this company. I had to sometimes challenge that because I felt that this was right on the margins of credibility and I didn't want to be associated with misleading information that wasn't painting a true picture of what was actually happening in the organisation. There were also times when I was put under pressure by the investor to get rid of somebody or reduce their salary. I often had to say that I wasn't going to do that because I didn't think that it was the proper course of action. In terms of integrity, I didn't want to endorse actions that I didn't think were appropriate.

Linda greatly appreciated the way in which he was able to chair meetings and defuse what would otherwise be very fraught situations. Despite there being difficult people on the board, she said that *'he never lost his temper or raised his voice, but he commanded the table'*. He expected people to compromise so that nobody expected to get their own way at someone else's expense.

After a period of successful acquisition and expansion, the company was approached by an American company, Ensign-Bickford Industries (EBI), who were heavily involved as analysts in the American grain market and who wanted to enter the United Kingdom agricultural analytical market. Because of its importance in the British market, Cawood Scientific was an obvious target. Waterland sold the company to EBI in 2021. EBI did not want a separate British board, and so the board of Cawood was disbanded in November of that year. Donald, Nigel and Linda were all forced to cut their ties with the company at that point.

Donald's stamina, passion and enthusiasm as well as his Christian concern for people had helped Cawood Scientific on its journey of maintaining its standing of being a very successful company providing an important service within the agricultural sector.

CHAPTER NINE

Fingers in Lots of Pies

Donald's reputation as a man of integrity who was able to get things done, and who held an in-depth knowledge of both the workings of agriculture and the machinery of government, meant that he was in great demand to sit on various bodies. In this chapter we shall look at Donald's involvement in some of these bodies and the influence that he had on them.

The Scottish Agricultural College

A key function of the Meat and Livestock Commission was to promote agricultural research so that the livestock industry would become more efficient. Donald chaired the Research Steering Committee to investigate how scientific research could further help the industry in areas such as genetics and management systems. The MLC allocated funding each year to contract with research institutions that would undertake the work it required. One of the key institutions involved in this work was the Scottish

Agricultural College (now known as Scotland's Rural College), and Donald worked alongside key scientists from the college, such as Professor Geoff Simm.

The Chair of the college board at that time was Dr Maitland Mackie, who was part of what is now a five-generation-old family whose first sons are all called Maitland. The family have farmed Westertown Farm in Aberdeenshire throughout all of these generations, and are now probably most famous as the producers of Mackie's Ice Cream, a premium ice cream brand.

Because of the importance of the college's role in agricultural research for the MLC, Maitland sat on the consultative committee that Donald established. He and Donald got on very well together, and indeed Donald found Maitland quite inspiring, saying:

Maitland was a remarkable man. He had a big brain. People used to joke about Maitland that he always has ten ideas going on at any one time. Two of them are brilliant, but the difficulty is identifying which two.

Maitland was a brilliant man, but with so much going on in his mind he sometimes forgot what were, to him, only trivial details. On one occasion when the company was doing an audit, they discovered that a car was missing. It was eventually reported to be at Edinburgh Airport. Maitland had left it there, flown off somewhere and then came back home by train, forgetting all about the car that he had left at the airport. It was suggested that the parking fee accumulated at the airport was greater than the value of the car!

Maitland admired Donald's skills as Chair of the MLC, and was desperate to get Donald to join the college board. Donald had to turn him down, as there would have been a conflict of interest if Donald were to sit on the board of an institution that was receiving payments for doing work for the MLC. As soon as Donald had retired from the MLC, Maitland was on the phone to ask him if he would now be available to join the board. Donald went up to visit the college and agreed to Maitland's request. He was a board member from 2001 to 2006, and Vice-Chair for about half of that time.

What Maitland had omitted to tell him was that relations between the board members and the college management team were very poor, with the college Chief Executive and the Chair of the board barely on speaking terms. Maitland was hoping that Donald, with all of his experience on different bodies and coming in fresh to the college, would be able to resolve these tensions and bring the two sides together. This did eventually happen, and replacing the Chief Executive Officer certainly helped, but it was hard work. As Donald put it, '*I hadn't experienced anything like it before I went up there.*'

Donald enjoyed his time on the board, as the work of the college fitted in with his interests. The educational side of the college was obviously important in training students in agriculture and latterly other rural studies. The science base for research was very strong, and the college had an excellent reputation for research across the United Kingdom. In addition, the college had a consultancy business, providing advice to farmers. Indeed, it was quite unique having these three strands operating from the one institution.

Despite the success of the college, there were the almost inevitable financial challenges that Donald and board members had to deal with. The three campuses that the college had in Edinburgh, Ayr and Aberdeen had originally been separate colleges, but as such they were unsustainable and had to be brought together into one college. Because of high overheads, a number of redundancies had to be made to put the college on to a more secure financial footing.

When Maitland Mackie decided to retire, he wanted Donald to become Chair in his place. There was, however, a major problem: Donald lived in England! The Scottish government was very supportive of the college and was a major source of funds. Because of that, requests for board membership had to go through the Holyrood government. Ross Finnie, the Minister for the Environment and Rural Development in the Scottish government, turned down this request, which upset the board, but they had to accept his decision.

Donald stepped down in 2006, having thoroughly enjoyed the service he had given to the college.

The National Land Based College

We noted in the previous section that the Scottish Agricultural College changed its name to Scotland's Rural College. This change of college classification took place across the whole country, as agricultural colleges became known as land based or rural colleges. The reason for this change was quite simple: there was less demand for agricultural courses, and so less income was being generated from these courses. Colleges were thus forced to diversify into broader land based courses, such as animal care (including dog grooming), equine studies, horticulture, environmental management and golf course management, as well as traditional courses in agriculture.

An overarching organisation, Landex (Land Based Colleges and Universities Aspiring to Excellence) was established in 2006 to represent the interests of land based colleges and the industries they served. At the time, Donald was Chair of NFU Mutual, and he was asked if the company could act as host for the official launch of Landex. In doing so he worked very closely with former Principal of Bishop Burton College in Yorkshire, Howard Petch, himself a committed Christian who had done much of the groundwork for the establishment of the organisation.

Donald was later approached by Chris Moody, the Chief Executive of Landex, to support a new body, the National Land Based College, that would authenticate qualifications across the land based sector. This college would be separate from Landex, but would work alongside it. The aim was to raise standards through a consistent approach to qualifications offered to students across all colleges. This would replace the rather fragmented system of different colleges offering different qualifications that were not standardised against each other. The national college would also act as a link between the colleges and government departments.

Donald agreed to chair initial meetings of a steering group to see if there was sufficient industry support for this to go ahead, and at this stage there did seem to be a fair amount of interest. Landex were prepared to put in substantial funding to set the college up and get it going. Donald and Chris Moody led the negotiations with the awarding body City and Guilds, who were brought in as a major partner to provide qualifications across the sector. A board was appointed, with Donald as Chair, and the college seemed ready to start business.

The scheme was promoted to all the individual colleges that were members of Landex. Donald assumed that because of the initial interest and the backing of Landex their college members would welcome the scheme and buy into it. This, however, was not to be the case. Some did, but others refused to change from their existing qualifications provider. As a result, after four or five years the national college struggled financially because there was not the widespread support that Donald thought there would be. Insufficient students were taking the approved qualifications to generate enough income to support the scheme. Landex took the scheme back in house, so although the national college still exists, it is under Landex's umbrella.

Donald decided to step down from the college board in 2017 because he felt the college had not had the national impact he thought it would have in raising standards. There have not been many undertakings led by Donald that have not achieved the success that he had hoped for, but the National Land Based College was certainly one of them. He does, however, remain as a Vice-President of

Landex and continues to be very supportive of the crucial role of the land based colleges.

The Countryside Classroom

One of Donald's passions is to encourage children and young people to develop a strong interest in farming and the processes involved in bringing food to our tables. He also wants them to understand issues related to the environment and the countryside, as well as the need for healthy eating to overcome our current problems of childhood obesity. Ultimately, he wanted more and more of these young people to see agriculture as an attractive career prospect. He wrote about this in the Policy Commission Report, making reference to organisations linking schools and farms, particularly Farming and Countryside Education (FACE). FACE was established by the National Farmers' Union (NFU) and the Royal Agricultural Society of England (RASE).

In the report, Donald praised the work of FACE in trying to bring schools and farms together, and the way in which NFU and RASE pooled their resources, a common theme in Donald's thinking:

We welcome this recognition that co-ordinating resources is a more effective way of getting messages across. We hope that more industry bodies will join the FACE initiative and help make a real impact on information provided to schools.[60]

---

60. *Farming and Food: A Sustainable Future* (2002), p. 99.

FACE was managed by Bill Graham, supported by Janet Higginbottom. Donald first met them at their stand at the Royal Show in 2002. Bill and Janet had no idea who he was, and that he was the person who had written so positively about their work in the Policy Commission Report. They were surprised and rather embarrassed when he identified himself. Subsequently they asked if he would chair a strategy group for FACE, which he agreed to do. Donald did what he could to support their work in schools and in arranging school visits to farms and the countryside.

Later, he called a meeting of all the groups involved in farming education liaison. Over twenty organisations turned up to the meeting, held in the Farmers' Club in Whitehall. Donald asked them all to give a two-minute briefing of what they did, and what impact they thought they were having. What they were doing seemed to be very impressive, but perhaps rather small-scale. He then asked them to come back to the next meeting with more concrete evidence of numbers and impact. When they came back and totals were added, it seemed that they were reaching about a million children (mostly primary), and although the evidence on impact was mostly anecdotal, they did believe that they were making a difference and influencing attitudes.

Donald's follow-up question was: '*Shouldn't you all be working much more closely together to collectively try and reach all children in primary schools? And what about secondary schools?*' They all gave this some thought and eventually committed themselves to creating a website for teachers called Countryside Classroom.[61] This is a plethora

---

61. https://www.countrysideclassroom.org.uk/ (accessed 7/4/25).

of resources for teachers to use in all curriculum areas and in all key stages. There are also links for possible farm visits that teachers may want to organise.

Donald's passion in this area and his persistence in bringing people together have led to the creation of an outstanding educational resource which teachers can easily use with their students. He still hosts an annual meeting of all the partner organisations involved in Countryside Classroom to review progress and agree future plans. These organisations continue to be very enthusiastic about the project, over twenty years after its inception.

The Set-Aside Group

In 1988 the European Union introduced a set-aside policy, whereby farmers were paid to take ten per cent of their cropland out of production. This policy was introduced to try to reduce the large food surpluses that had accumulated as a result of overproduction. Environmental groups welcomed this policy, as they saw the benefit of not spreading chemicals on ten per cent of the land, as well as providing land for ground-nesting birds.

By the beginning of the new millennium, the surpluses had diminished as a result of an increase in the global demand for cereals, accompanied by a rise in world food prices. The EU now felt that with a changed economic climate, set-aside should be abolished. Farming bodies, such as the National Farmers' Union and the Country Land and Business Association, were pleased because they could now plough up this set-aside land and sow cereal crops, which they could sell for much higher prices. Environmental bodies, such as the Environment Agency, Natural England and the Royal Society for the Protection of Birds, were very much against abolition, fearing the loss of benefits to the environment and wildlife. Thus there was a real tension between the two groups.

Hilary Benn was Secretary of State at the time, and he had to bring about some resolution. He felt that there was only one person who could bring the two groups together, and that of course was Donald. The Set-Aside Group, as it was called, was established in 2007 with representatives of the farming and environmental lobbies under Donald's chairmanship. The differences of opinion within the room during their first meeting led Henry Aubrey-Fletcher, President of the Country Land and Business Association, to comment afterwards, *'Well, that was an experience, Don. If I was wearing a pacemaker, it would be fully charged.'*

From the outset, Donald realised that he was going to have a difficult challenge in bringing the two groups together to reach a solution. He told the delegates at the first meeting:

Now, you do realise, all of you, that there is not going to be one side victorious out of all of this, and one side defeated. You are all going to have to consider how you compromise to reach an agreement. There are only two possible solutions. One is that you are all going to be equally happy, and the other is that you are all equally unhappy. You need to think about that if we are going to reach an agreement.

The group had regular meetings to try to push things forward, and after about nine months they eventually came to a compromise solution. Donald had during the course of these meetings put forward a proposal of voluntary set-aside, whereby farmers, if they wished, could set aside some of their land for wildlife conservation, but there would be no compulsion to do so. There was some haggling over what percentage was to be recommended, but it was finally decided to settle on a voluntary set-aside of five per cent. They had finally reached agreement! Donald summed up the experience saying:

> *It was one of the toughest sets of negotiations that I have been involved in, trying to find a solution when you had two immovable forces, neither of which wanted to give way at all. Certainly from the earlier meetings, there was no way that they were going to compromise. But we got an agreement in the end, and Hilary Benn was very pleased.*

The Agricultural Forum

The Agricultural Forum is an elite group of members drawn from the agricultural community and related sectors, with the aim of debating aspects of agricultural policy. Although it was originally set up by the National Farmers' Union and the Country Land and Business Association, it was not intended as an organisation to take specific action, but rather to be a talking, listening and learning community. Meetings take place three or four times each year, each with a guest speaker and an excellent dinner.

The membership is limited to thirty-six, and if a vacancy arises, a new member is voted on by other members of the forum. Donald's membership was proposed by Ben Gill. In 2011 he was approached by the Chair John Gummer (previously Environment Secretary) and the previous Chair Nicholas Saphir (formerly the Chair of Food from Britain) and asked if he would be willing to become Forum Chair. Donald held the Chair until 2018.

One of his main tasks as Chair was to find interesting speakers for the regular meetings of the forum. This was not an easy task, but Donald produced an array of good speakers, including government ministers, ambassadors and chairs of companies, public sector bodies and regulators, such as the Environment Agency. Many of these people came to speak at forum meetings because of the respect that they had for Donald. Hilary Benn, Secretary of State for Food, Environment and Rural Affairs, having been told that it was a great honour to have him at the meeting replied by saying, *'Well, if Don Curry asks, how can you refuse?'*

For the thirty-six members of the forum, the meetings provided lots of relevant information and food for thought, which they were able to take back to their respective farming groups.

The Royal Veterinary College

Donald and Rhoda were standing on the platform of the railway station at Doncaster, having attended the funeral of his last surviving uncle, Ian Hunter.[62] His phone rang and

---

62. Ian had been a bank manager who had complained of ill health all of his life, retired at the age of fifty-five, but survived to the very old age of ninety-three.

it was Gillian Shephard, who had been a former Minister of Agriculture, Fisheries and Food in the early 1990s. She told Donald that she had just the job for him, to take over from her as Chair of the council of the Royal Veterinary College. Rhoda's response was: *'Chair of the Royal Veterinary College? You can't be serious! You haven't got a degree and are not a vet!'*

Before committing himself, he agreed to meet with other board members and the Principal, Professor Stuart Reid. When he met with them, he wanted to find out more about the college, but of course at the same time they were looking at him to see if he would make a suitable Chair. He must have satisfied them, because they offered him the post.

There was no question of Donald not accepting this position (despite Rhoda's incredulity), as he had always held the veterinary profession in high regard. He remembers from his teenage years Gerald Curry, a vet from Alnwick who was also a cousin of his father, Rob, coming to the family farm at Low Burradon to tend to their sick animals. Whenever Gerald came, he would regale the family with amusing stories from his experience as a vet. One such story was about a client who was looking for straight answers from him. The client instructed him next time to send *'a one-handed vet'* as he was fed up being told, *'on the one hand you could do this, or on the other hand ...'*

Of course, when he was Chair of the MLC he was greatly indebted to the veterinary profession as they struggled to understand the nature of BSE and what action could be taken to mitigate its effects. Having Colin Maclean as his Director General was a real blessing for Donald, as Colin had practical experience as a veterinary surgeon and worked very closely with the Chief Veterinary Officers at the time, Keith Meldrum followed by James Scudamore.

Therefore, taking up the role of chairing the Royal Veterinary College (RVC) was an opportunity that Donald could not turn down. He began his role as Chair in 2012, a position he held for seven years. He viewed his appointment as a tremendous privilege. As he himself put it:

What an incredible honour for a non-academic to be appointed to chair the oldest and most prestigious veterinary school in the English-speaking world!

The Royal Veterinary College (RVC) is a stand-alone college, but has a federated relationship with the University of London, with two campuses: one in Camden in London and one at Hawkshead in Hertfordshire. Its beginnings relate to a racehorse called Eclipse that was never beaten on the racecourse in 1769 and 1770, and then was retired until his death in 1789. Racing enthusiasts at the time wanted to know why Eclipse had been so successful and the ultimate cause of his death. There was no veterinary school in the country at the time, and there were no English veterinarians who could answer these questions. The only person who could do so was a Frenchman called Charles de St Bel, who was able to present his findings on Eclipse. More significantly, de St Bel wished to establish a veterinary school in England, and he was assisted in this by members of the Odiham Agricultural Society that existed to promote the knowledge and understanding of animal husbandry. Together they founded the London Veterinary

College in February 1791, on the present Camden site of the college.

The college grew from these small beginnings to become a very large, highly successful veterinary college that is recognised globally for its high standards in research, teaching and clinical services.[63] Donald was proud to be associated with a college that was ranked number one amongst veterinary colleges worldwide twice during his tenure. He enjoyed presiding over graduation services, seeing large numbers of successful young people launching on to their new careers in the veterinary world, as well as hosting the college's two hundred and twenty-fifth anniversary celebrations.

He also worked with the principal, Stuart Reid, to improve the college's financial performance, which had been rather alarming when he started, until they got to the position where they could make significant investments in teaching, research and recreational facilities, as well as student accommodation, which was necessary because of the high costs of living in London. Princess Anne twice visited the college to open new facilities, and was particularly interested in the college's equine research.

Stuart saw him, as so many others have done, as being an outstanding Chair:

The meeting was run with military precision; I think that I was in only one meeting that overran. He just seemed to have an awareness of how to move things

---

63. Ranking is carried out by the QS World University Rankings. Indeed in 2025, the college was ranked number one in the world for the fifth year in a row (*Vet Record*, 29th March 2025).

on . . . he always steered us through it, and he always gave people, including the more junior members and the slightly less well informed, the opportunity to comment. He was very good at understanding the breadth of the agenda that we were trying to cover. He also understood good governance, and so, for example, Don didn't sit on any of the subcommittees, as he trusted the chairs of the subcommittees to get on with their business and then bring matters back to the top table. He felt that if he was in there, people might defer to him, he might influence people, and he would end up with two bites of the cake.

He had a very good relationship with Stuart, who saw him as a friend and mentor with a wonderful sense of humour. Stuart also recalled the colourful socks that he wore, which endeared him to the college staff.

It was the tragedy of Jane's death, as described in chapter two, that cemented their relationship. Donald and Rhoda were very touched that Stuart took the time to come up to Newcastle for her funeral. Stuart put it this way:

When Donald lost his daughter, I didn't hesitate for a minute to know that I should go and represent the college at the funeral. It was a bleak, bleak day on a Northumberland hillside in the graveyard. But even in his grief with the hundreds of people that were there, he found his way across to speak to me and say thank you. I was not expecting that. That was a bonding moment for us. That was Donald; he always looked to the wider community.

Donald thoroughly enjoyed the time that he spent serving the college. He felt, however, that under the governance arrangements that he helped to establish, he should stand down in August 2019. He was made a Fellow of the RVC in July 2022.

The Institute of Agriculture and Horticulture

In the years after his disappointment over the lack of influence that the National Land Based College had in raising the standards of education and training, Donald had a continuing frustration that the agricultural sector was not adequately promoting itself as an industry. There seemed to be, for example, no central place for young people to obtain information about careers in farming. Other industries and professions had institutes that would provide central careers advice and thus signpost people to courses available and the necessary entry requirements. Nobody seemed to be promoting agriculture.

Other people felt the same as Donald, two of whom were Judith Batchelar of the major supermarket chain Sainsbury's, and John Shropshire of G's, one of the largest horticultural growers in the country. With their support, he decided to establish a senior leadership group to take their ideas forward. Donald chaired this group, and from there they organised a large conference for the industry at Stoneleigh in Warwickshire, where they had a number of sessions discussing the skills deficits in the industry, and how they might be overcome. Donald chaired the closing session of the conference, and he was told, *'Just get on with it. We'll support you. We need a more professional front.'*

This support from the industry enabled Donald to approach his contacts in government to seek financial assistance. Endorsement from this group was necessary for DEFRA to support the organisation financially without needing to obtain competitive tenders. A detailed business plan was drawn up in order to obtain government approval. Donald established a consultation group, which enabled him to meet regularly with the Chairs and Chief Executives of the main agricultural organisations to obtain their guidance and support. As in other organisations that he supported, he was able to get key people round the table. Tim Mordan, a Deputy Director with DEFRA at the time who worked with Donald on this project, said, *'Donald's USP* [unique selling point] *is in bringing the right people together.'*

In 2020 the senior leadership group formed a Development Board that Donald asked David Fursdon to chair to take the project forward. David was a friend of Donald, a former President of the Country Land and Business Association, and the person who replaced Donald on the board of the Crown Estate. In November 2020 DEFRA committed financial support to what was to be called The Institute of Agriculture and Horticulture (TIAH).

TIAH's aims, as set out on its website are to:

Embed a culture of lifelong learning and continuous professional development;
Drive greater uptake of training;
Promote agriculture and horticulture as a progressive, professional and exciting career choice.[64]

---

64.   https://tiah.org/about-us (accessed 10.11.24).

One of the key tools to support lifelong learning is the National Library for Agri-Food, initially established through Food and Farming Futures. As mentioned in the previous chapter, TIAH took over the operation of the library in 2024, and so it now sits in its rightful place at the heart of the industry.

Donald never intended to continue leading the institute, so he stepped down from the senior leadership group. He continues, however, to chair meetings of the consultation group twice a year, and he has been made a Patron of TIAH.

The Better Regulation Executive

As we saw in chapter six, Donald was described as an 'honorary minister' as he oversaw the implementation of the recommendations of his policy commission into the future of farming and food. He enjoyed working at the heart of government, but he decided to stand down from this role in the latter half of 2009. An election was due, and he could not be sure that an incoming government would welcome his presence as an 'honorary minister'.

He did, however, see an advertisement that took his interest; it was for the role of Chair of the Better Regulation Executive (BRE). This executive was established in 2005 with the aim of monitoring and reducing the whole plethora of regulatory burdens that were placed on organisations in the private, public and voluntary sectors. Many of these regulations serve an excellent purpose in protecting public welfare, but too many of these bureaucratic regulations went back decades (and even centuries), and were often no longer relevant in protecting people's rights, health and safety. Bureaucratic red tape that serves no useful purpose results in high costs for organisations that endeavour to comply with it. Therefore, a balance has to be maintained between removing costly regulations and the protection of the general public.

For Donald this role would be interesting because he would still be involved in the machinery of government. The subject matter would, however, be quite new to him as his experience to date had been largely limited to agriculture. He decided to go ahead and apply for the post, leaving it to God to grant it to him if it was his will. Much to Donald's surprise, he got an interview and was invited to meet with Sir Simon Fraser, the Permanent Secretary for the Department for Business. He was successful and was appointed to the post on 1st January 2010.

Labour was still in power then, and Lord Peter Mandelson was President of the Board of Trade with ministerial responsibility for the Better Regulation Executive. Donald met with him not long after he started his role. It would seem, however, that Lord Mandelson was more interested in talking about Donald's farm, admitting that he would love to own a farm. Eventually they got on to the subject of regulation, with Lord Mandelson asking Donald, 'What are we going to do with this government and its attitude to regulation? They seem to regulate far too much.' This was a shock for Donald to hear, as Lord Mandelson was supposed to be the minister responsible for better regulation.

Donald got stuck into his role, with a team of about fifty civil servants working for him. It was a steep learning curve, with a whole new terminology that he had to get to grips with. There seemed to be a whole industry around impact assessments with the Regulatory Policy Committee assessing, for example, the economic impact or the environmental impact of each regulation proposed by different government departments. In each department, one of the ministers had responsibility for BRE, and Donald decided that he should meet with each of these ministers regularly. Donald's opening comment at these initial meetings with each minister was: '*I know that somewhere towards the bottom of your list of ministerial responsibilities is Better Regulation. My task is to elevate that topic to somewhere near the top.*'

In May 2010 Gordon Brown's Labour government lost the General Election and they were replaced by a Conservative-Liberal Democrat coalition government. Vince Cable, a Liberal Democrat Member of Parliament, became Secretary of State for Business, Innovation and Skills. Donald met with him, and he almost had an exact rerun of the conversation that he had had with Lord Mandelson six months earlier; the minister was very interested in Donald's farm, as he and his wife had a small cattle farm (and he knew about the intricacies of tagging the ears of calves!).

Oliver Letwin, a Cabinet Office Minister, also had responsibility and Donald described him as a '*terrier*' in trying to get the regulatory burden on businesses reduced. In a survey carried out with businesses, it was quite clear, and indeed almost inevitable, that they felt that regulation

169

was limiting their growth. This gave Donald and his ministerial bosses a clear mandate to try to make life easier for businesses. He set up a consultation group with business leaders to seek their advice and counsel. Donald himself learned a lot from working with groups such as the Confederation of British Industry, the Federation of Small Businesses, the Institute of Directors and the Chamber of Commerce.

In discussion with departments, he suggested to them that they did not always need to impose regulations but rather that they should look for alternative solutions, including seeing if businesses could solve problems themselves. Departments were asked to audit the regulations and accompanying guidance notes that they had, with the aim of reducing and simplifying the bureaucracy imposed on organisations. They were told that if they intended to introduce a new regulation that would impose a burden amounting to a certain value on business, they should simultaneously abolish a regulation of the same value, and so effectively it was 'one in, one out'. Oliver Letwin in terrier mode wanted to go further and be even more ambitious by introducing 'one in, two out'. A league table of departments was established, ranking them on their success in reducing regulations and on the quality of their impact assessments.

Donald also had discussions with regulatory bodies to try to get them to adopt a new approach, so that rather than beating businesses into submission if a business failed to meet a regulatory requirement, they should give them advice and assistance in order to become compliant. He wanted to change the culture of regulators. Also, he wanted to change the business culture so that companies would want to work with regulators to provide evidence to show that they are trying to be compliant. He felt that overall a lot of progress was made in creating a more harmonious culture between regulators and businesses.

One of the government departments that came low down in the league tables was the Home Office. This important state department covers a wide number of areas, including national security, policing, prisons, counterterrorism and immigration, and is very difficult to run. Indeed, a senior civil servant in a quote infamously but wrongly attributed to former Home Secretary John Reid, said in 2006, 'The Home Office is not fit for purpose.' Theresa May was Home Secretary in the time that Donald chaired the BRE, and she did not seem to have much interest in his work. After she became Prime Minister in 2016, this lack of interest was apparent, and, as a result, the BRE lost much of its momentum. Donald felt that it was now time to stand down. He was not replaced and all the work went in-house and so was no longer independent of government.

As Donald does whenever he takes on a particular responsibility, he has a great influence on the organisation. This was true with regard to regulation, which resulted in a cultural change in many government departments and the working of many regulators. Donald was convinced that his efforts had reduced the regulatory pressures on businesses and much had been achieved, but that the momentum needed to continue well beyond his term in office.

The Rural Design Centre

Donald has spent much of his public life working in London and elsewhere across the country on various projects, away from his beloved Northumberland. In more recent years, however, he has come back to serve his home area in different projects. One of the most prominent is the Rural Design Centre.

In October 2018 Simon Green, the CEO of Innovation SuperNetwork, approached Donald to see if he would be willing to chair an exploratory meeting with all the key regional bodies, to explore the main issues that impact on rural communities and rural businesses in the north-east of England. Simon had previously met Donald at an innovation event at Newcastle University on agri-foods, and when thinking about who could be a suitable Chair for this meeting, Donald came to mind, as Simon remembered how knowledgeable he was in this area and how open he was to innovation. Simon believed that Donald would be able to bring the right people together and ensure that they were going in the right direction.

Donald agreed to chair a meeting of regional bodies, with the first meeting of this advisory group taking place in November 2018. They decided to research the issues by talking to key stakeholders, such as the National Farmers' Union, the Country Land and Business Association, the Environment Agency, Northumbrian Water and the local authorities, and then bringing their findings together. The group agreed that a formal structure should be established.

The Rural Design Centre (RDC) was incorporated in December 2019 and officially started operating on 1st

January 2020, partnering with county councils, community groups and other bodies across the north-east, and with Donald as Chair of the board. At about the same time, Newcastle University had established a National Innovation Centre for Rural Enterprise (NICRE) that became involved in developing rural enterprise projects across the country. Simon and Donald decided to work closely with them, and established a formal agreement to work with the university on projects funded by European and other bodies. With the whole range of partners they formed the Rural Catalyst Partnership.

Their website explains the aim of the RDC:

> As part of the Rural Catalyst partnership with the National Innovation Centre for Rural Enterprise, the Centre delivers design-led projects with rural communities, bringing together community groups with businesses, researchers and public authorities. We spark collaboration among individuals, communities, businesses, researchers and policy-makers using design. Our shared ambition is a future where rural communities lead in innovation, resilience and sustainable growth.[65]

The emphasis is very much on communities collaborating with other organisations to come up with innovative, sustainable solutions to rural problems. Donald has involved himself in chairing conferences and meetings to help make this happen. Some of the initiatives have been very successful, such as the Community Energy Project in Northumberland using village halls and churches to

---

65.   https://www.ruraldesigncentre.com/about (accessed 9/5/25).

generate solar power. Another project in Northumberland aims to provide power to the three hundred and sixty rural households that are not served at all by the National Grid. Enterprising North is designed to support individuals in the rural communities of Northumberland and Gateshead who are looking to start their own business, or who are in their first six months of trading.

The organisation has grown remarkably since its inception in 2019. Simon has stepped down as part-time CEO to concentrate on his innovation consultancy work, and Paul Cowie has been appointed as a full-time replacement. Donald continues to chair the board.

Simon has appreciated the work that Donald has put into the centre. When Simon first contacted him, Donald had to warn him that he was very busy and would not be able to give much time to the project. As Simon said, however, 'Once he gets into it, he just can't help himself.' Simon believed that Donald brought credibility to the whole concept, and that his name and active involvement in the project started conversations. He was able to identify the right people to be involved through his many contacts. His immense knowledge of rural northern communities helped move the centre in the right direction. In chairing meetings, he was, as ever, very good at bringing stakeholders with different perspectives together to agree on measures that would be of benefit to local communities in the longer term. At a personal level, Simon appreciated the encouragement that Donald gave him on what would otherwise be quite a lonely journey.

The Rural Design Centre is a remarkable example of how local initiative in rural communities can be harnessed in collaboration with others to bring about sustainable change, something that, as we have seen, is very close to Donald's heart.

PART THREE

Charity

CHAPTER TEN

At Home in the Community

Jane's Legacy

On the afternoon of 16th September 2013 Jesmond Parish Church in Newcastle was filled with family and friends gathered together to say farewell to Jane Curry who had passed away eight days before. Donald and Rhoda were on holiday in Croatia when they received an urgent phone call to say that their beloved daughter Jane had succumbed to pneumonia, and was not expected to live. They flew home straightaway, and were given a precious twenty-four hours with Jane before she died. The funeral service in Jesmond allowed the gathering to thank God for the life of this remarkable lady, who despite her many disabilities had a massive influence on the lives of those gathered that afternoon.

Rev. Jonathan Redfearn, one of the church ministers, led the service, and the congregation heartily sang hymns of praise to the God who provides hope in all circumstances, including death.

David Bentley, Chair of the charity Prospects, had sent Donald an anonymous poem that he had come across. During the service, Jane's niece Eleanor,[66] who was only fifteen at the time, read this very moving poem, the words of which captured so much of the essence of Jane. The poem began:

I am the child who cannot talk.
You often pity me, I see it in your eyes.
You wonder how much I am aware of – I see that as well.
I am aware of much, whether you are happy or sad
or fearful,
patient or impatient, full of love and desire,
or if you are just doing your duty by me.
I marvel at your frustration, knowing mine to be
far greater,
for I cannot express myself or my needs as you do.

The poem continues with the child describing things that they cannot do, but nonetheless they are able through their disabilities to give so much to others. It finishes:

I am the disabled child.
I am your teacher. If you will allow me,
I will teach you what is really important in life.
I will give you and teach you unconditional love.
I gift you my innocent trust, my dependency upon you.
I teach you about how precious this life is and about
not taking things for granted.
I teach you about forgetting your own needs and
desires and dreams.

---

66. This was Eleanor whose marriage Donald referred to in his interview with Tim Farron as mentioned in chapter six.

I teach you giving.
Most of all I teach you hope and faith.
I am the disabled child.[67]

Bos Menzies, a pastor who had been Managing Director of At Home in the Community for a number of years, preached the sermon in which he talked about the legacy that Jane had left. Despite her disabilities and her inability to talk, she had touched the lives of so many people. Those who knew her well, or even those who had just met her on some occasion, would not be able to forget this remarkable lady. Many who had not met her at all owed so much to her through the charity At Home in the Community, which Donald and Rhoda helped to establish to support young people like Jane. That is indeed a wonderful legacy.

As we saw in chapter two, Donald and Rhoda had found a place for Jane at Stelling Hall near Stocksfield when she was fourteen years old and increasingly difficult to look after at home. Stelling Hall was one of the National Children's Homes, an organisation originally founded by Methodist minister Thomas Bowman Stephenson. It continued to have links with the Methodist Church and so had quite a strong Christian ethos. She was well looked after there, but by the time she reached her early twenties and deemed to be an adult, Donald and Rhoda had to find another place for her.

Jane attended Priory Special School in Hexham (and thereafter the Adult Learning Centre in Hexham). There were a number of the Priory School parents like Donald and

---

67. To read the whole poem, refer to Gavin's Voice website (18th February 2008) http://gavins-voice.blogspot.com/2008/02/i-am-child-author-unknown.html (accessed 23.4.24).

Rhoda who were very concerned about what would happen to their sons and daughters as they got older. In addition, a group of Christian parents began to meet together after they had heard a talk in Newcastle given by David Potter, an inspirational Baptist minister from Reading.

David and his wife Madeleine had a daughter, Rachel, who had Down's syndrome. In the 1960s and '70s they discovered that there were very few resources to help parents of children like Rachel. In particular, there were very few Christian resources to help Christian parents. The Potters also realised that there were lots of Christian parents who wanted to find a secure Christian environment for their children with learning disabilities. This propelled David to set up Prospects (originally called A Cause for Concern) in 1976 as a charity that would provide support for people with learning disabilities to live in Christian homes.[68]

The group approached David to ask if he could open a home in the north-east. He regrettably declined, feeling that his organisation did not have the capacity to expand northwards, but he said that he would be prepared to give advice. This was of course not the response that the group wanted to hear, but Donald, Rhoda and the others felt that God was leading them to start up their own organisation.

The Beginnings of At Home in the Community

Donald was asked to chair the working group, and Peter Stoner, a fine Christian man who was a member of

---

68. To read more about Rachel and the establishment of Prospects, refer to David Potter's article in *Evangelicals Now*, 24th January 2013. https://evangelicalsnow.wordpress.com/2013/01/24/promise-fulfilled-david-potter-celebrates-the-life-of-his-daughter-rachel/ (accessed 18.4.24).

Ambassador Hall Assembly in Walker, Newcastle, became Secretary. After lots of discussion and undertaking lots of research, they set up a charity that they named At Home in the Community and had registered as a charity in February 1990. Donald became Chair of the charity board.

It was important that as a charity they worked with local authority social services departments to ensure that they fulfilled legal standards. This was an opportune time for them to get themselves established, as it was now government policy to close down long-stay mental hospitals and endeavour to have clients receive care in the community. At Home in the Community was well placed to carry out that mission.

The group had very helpful discussions with Brian Roycroft, Director of Social Services for Newcastle City Council, a local authority officer who was highly respected and held in high regard for his care for the vulnerable in the community. As Donald said:

> *Brian Roycroft was willing to take a risk on us. We had no track record, we had never run a home, we knew nothing about the management of residential homes, but he was willing with his team to take a risk and support At Home.*

The most difficult hurdle they faced in negotiating with the social services team was in convincing them that as a Christian organisation they did not pose a risk to the people they would be looking after. The team was concerned that Donald and his colleagues would end up indoctrinating the residents and not allow them to have necessary treatments, such as blood transfusions. To Donald, '*it was appalling really that our Christian ethos was seen as risky, when in fact it should have been seen as a really positive move that we were only in this for the benefit of the residents, and we had no ulterior motive'.*

Donald and his colleagues were able to overcome this hurdle, and as a result of negotiations with the council team, they opened their first house in the Walker area of Newcastle in 1992. Sue Laidler, who was Manager of Stelling Hall where Jane was a resident, was appointed Manager of the house in Walker. Sue applied for the post because she wanted to work for an organisation with a strong Christian ethos, as she felt that her current employer, National Children's Homes, was slipping away from its Christian roots.

The first residents were two young men who had lived in the local community and three ladies who had come from a mental hospital in Prudhoe. The positive, and indeed remarkable, effects of being in the home in Walker were soon evident. For example, the mother of one of the ladies had told them that she used to talk a bit before going into Prudhoe Hospital. The At Home team checked with the hospital staff who were quite definite that for twenty years there, she had never said a word. Within three months of being in the house, however, she amazingly started to talk again.

The first house was very significant for the board. As Donald said:

This was where we cut our teeth. We learned lessons in how to run homes for people with disabilities, engaging with local authorities and social services, and all the networks that surround them.

After the opening of the first house, the board looked for opportunities elsewhere in the north-east. Donald and Rhoda, along with other Priory School parents, were keen to have a house in Hexham, to accommodate young adults like Jane. The Director of Social Services for Northumberland, however, was not as helpful as Brian Roycroft had been in Newcastle, and indeed at the meeting with parents, some of the mothers were reduced to tears as he did not seem to be willing to solve their problems. Donald went back to see him and the two of them came to an agreement. The Director wanted a house to be opened in the small town of Haltwhistle, about fifteen miles to the west of Hexham, and so it was agreed that if Donald opened a home there and was able to obtain a suitable property in Hexham, he would be allowed to open both homes. That is what they did, opening both homes and accommodating five residents in each house, so that both the Director and the Hexham parents (including Donald and Rhoda) were pleased with the final outcome. Jane moved into the house in Hallgate in Hexham in 1992, along with four other residents.

Donald brought others onto the board, men and women of Christian faith and integrity who could provide particular expertise and thus meet a skills gap in the running of the charity. One such Director was Ian Simpson, who was brought on in 2004 because of his financial acumen gained through many years of banking experience. Ian and Donald worked closely together, and Ian became Vice-Chair, very much appreciating Donald's committed leadership:

I was always amazed, given how much else he had going on, just how much time he was willing to commit to At Home in the Community.

Over a twenty-year period At Home opened homes in a number of north-eastern towns, largely following their original model. They also supported individuals in Newcastle and Gateshead. By 2014 there were forty-four adults registered as users of At Home services, cared for by one hundred and thirty staff. After the last Care Quality Commission inspection looking into the work of At Home as a separate organisation, the charity received a good report, showing that it was clearly meeting the expected standards.[69]

Challenges

At Home in the Community met the needs of many vulnerable adults, and Donald certainly felt that this was 'a work of God'. There were, however, challenges and disappointments along the way. One lay in working with local churches. Donald felt that churches should be involved in supporting the work, but sadly there were not strong links with local churches, although individual Christians did support the residents by visiting them and taking them out, which was greatly appreciated. In addition, Christians got involved with the charity as directors.

Recruiting and retaining staff was another key issue. The charity relied on payments from the local authorities

---

69.   https://www.cqc.org.uk/location/1-719589911 (accessed 23.4.24).

to meet the costs of running the homes, particularly the payment of staff. The funding deals with both Newcastle and Northumberland were initially fine and largely covered the costs of running the homes. Over time, however, budgets were squeezed and inflationary increases were not passed on. The cost of meeting new regulations, such as those associated with safeguarding, were rising, putting the charity's finances under increasing pressure.

Supporters did raise money through fundraising ventures, such as taking part in the Great North Run and the Three Peaks Challenge, where about twenty people amazingly climbed Ben Nevis, Scafell Pike and Snowdon in twenty-four hours.

Donald and Rhoda opened their garden each year to the public to raise funds. Before the event, Donald would spend weeks getting the garden ready by ensuring that not a single weed was to be seen, and that the rose bushes and flower beds were perfect. One year, when the day came it was foggy, very damp and unpleasant. As cars arrived from all directions, drivers would comment that the sun had been shining when they left home. It seemed that the sun was shining everywhere in the vicinity, apart from Middle Farm. As a result, most people just stayed in the marquee, drinking tea and eating cakes. Donald concluded:

I decided that God was teaching me a lesson. My garden had become an idol and I needed to keep it in perspective.

Despite all of these herculean fundraising efforts, the board were not able to pay any more than the minimum wage to their staff, which was not enough in Donald's eyes to reward them for the dedicated service that most of them gave. A number of staff continued working for the charity out of love for the adults they looked after and out of loyalty to the organisation, but others felt that they could not afford to work for such a low payment, given their own financial commitments. At one stage there was roughly a twenty per cent staff turnover, making consistent, continuous care very difficult to maintain. Of course, as staff left, it became increasingly hard to recruit new high-quality staff. Donald would have liked to appoint more Christian staff, but unfortunately not enough Christians applied for posts.

It seemed that the work of the charity was no longer financially sustainable, which is sadly a common experience for small organisations in the care sector. Donald wanted to ensure that everything was done in a proper way, and that the operation of the charity would be a Christian witness to others. He and the board needed to look at other options. They decided to go back to Prospects from whom they had received so much help in the early days, and a merger was agreed, with Donald taking on the role of Vice-Chair of Prospects. A merger made sense as a larger organisation would be more able to absorb increasing overheads. It was not the case, however, of At Home simply being swallowed up by a bigger organisation; many of the working practices of At Home were adopted by Prospects as they were recognised as excellent practice.

In May 2016 Prospects itself merged with Livability, another Christian charity that supported those with disabilities, and which had grown out of the nineteenth-century charity the Shaftesbury Society. Donald is currently Vice-President of Livability (renamed Shaftesbury in 2024 reflecting its roots), and is pleased that the original work of At Home in the Community is continuing within a strong Christian ethos. Most of the original houses are still open, including the one in Hexham where Jane had lived. Jane's legacy very much lives on.

Thoughts of An Elderly Aunt

As we mentioned in chapter five, in 2001 Donald was given a knighthood for his services to agriculture. Seven years later in April 2008, he was given an honorary degree of Doctor of Civil Law by his local university, the University of Newcastle.[70] At the ceremony, Professor Patrick Chinnery, a neurologist, spoke about Donald's many achievements serving the nation by reshaping the agricultural industry. He spoke, for example, about his work with the NFU and NFU Mutual for the benefit of the farming community, and how he became Chair of the Meat and Livestock Commission at *an exceptionally young age*.[71] He went on to say that Donald chaired the Policy Commission and within five months produced his report – *'something of a miracle for a government document'*.

Looking at Donald's professional achievements, Professor Chinnery was able to say:

---

70. Quotations are taken from the transcript of the speeches made at the Honorary Degrees Congregation at Newcastle University on 11th April 2008.
71. Donald was just a few days away from his fiftieth birthday when he was confirmed as Chair. Whether that was exceptionally young or not depends on where you are standing. Tony Blair was four days away from his forty-fourth birthday when he became Prime Minister. Perhaps the 1990s was a time when relatively young people were given more freedom to take on major responsibilities.

*Despite his position and influence, his colleagues
describe him as a man of great humility, who has,
through his actions, secured the trust of the whole
industry, inspiring loyalty in friends and colleagues.
What better person could have chaired the Meat and
Livestock Commission through the BSE crisis?*

Professor Chinnery felt that nobody in Donald's professional
circles could have disagreed with the decision to give him
a knighthood for his work in helping to rescue agriculture
from a grave crisis. The professor revealed, however, that
somebody did disagree with the decision, somebody close
to home. It was Aunt Ella, one of Rhoda's elderly aunts,
who had doubts not about Donald receiving a knighthood,
but rather about what the knighthood was honouring.[72]

What Aunt Ella was asking was: '*Why was his knighthood
not for At Home in the Community?*' The professor went
on to explain to the gathering what the At Home charity
aimed to achieve and how significant it was for many
vulnerable people in the community. He explained how
important Donald's role in the charity was:

*Against all the odds, Sir Donald was instrumental in
establishing At Home in the Community. His close
colleagues tell me that this was only possible because
he holds his local charitable work on equal footing*

---

72. When Donald received his knighthood, Aunt Ella wanted to be sure that Donald would
remember whom he was serving and to have the right priorities in his life. She wanted
Rhoda to pass on the verse of the old hymn written by Katherine Hankey in 1866:
Tell me the same old story
When you have cause to fear
That this world's empty glory
Is costing me too dear.
Donald has always felt that these were wise, spiritual words that he constantly needed
to apply to his life.

with his work at a national level – frequently hopping off the flight from Heathrow straight into a meeting in the voluntary sector.

Professor Chinnery understood the importance of Donald's faith as a motivating force in his charitable work:

His conviction is underpinned by a deep personal faith, which he shares with others as a lay preacher.

Donald received his honorary degree for both his outstanding contribution to British farming and his '*equally important charitable work in Northumberland*'.

Perhaps that was thanks to Aunt Ella!

CHAPTER ELEVEN

The Prince's Countryside Fund

Donald and the Prince of Wales[73]

As we have seen in previous chapters, His Royal Highness the Prince of Wales was a strong support in Donald's work as Chair of the Meat and Livestock Commission and Chair of the Policy Commission. For example, he worked with Donald in rebuilding confidence in British beef during the BSE crisis by hosting dinners and meetings with top European chefs. He also hosted a visit of the Policy Commission and gave his advice on how the agricultural industry could move forward. After Donald's work on these two bodies was finished, he continued to meet with the Prince to discuss agricultural policy. The Prince was deeply concerned about the decline of the countryside, rural depopulation, the loss of traditional agricultural skills and the demise of family farms, which he felt represented the culture of agriculture. He and Donald had many

---

73. The Prince of Wales, since his accession to the throne on 8th September 2022, is now of course His Majesty King Charles III. We shall in this chapter refer to him by the title Prince of Wales, as he was known during the years that Donald worked with him, apart from in the quotes from Elizabeth Buchanan, who consistently referred to him as the King.

conversations about what might be done to support the farming community and restore the rural way of life.

These two men with a deep passion for agriculture got on very well together. Elizabeth Buchanan, the Prince's Private Secretary, initially brought them together during Donald's time as MLC Chair, as she had known of him in her previous role at Bell Pottinger, a company that did public relations work for the MLC. Elizabeth continued to be the link between the Prince and Donald over the years, and saw how well they worked together. She commented:

> *Don had such a terrific way with him. I've seen lots of people who work with the King, and there are some people who get it right and some people who get it wrong. The thing about Don is that he is consistent, courteous, wise, thoughtful and understated. Don's life is about service and duty, and that is the King's life, and his deep faith helps in this.*

These conversations usually took place in Clarence House and at Highgrove, but one took place in one of the Prince's residences in Scotland, Birkhall, the former home of his grandmother, Queen Elizabeth the Queen Mother. This particular meeting involved a drive through treacherous wintry conditions, with Donald accompanied by Elizabeth Buchanan. She well recalled the journey, which started off with a flight to Aberdeen:

> *We set off. Everything was fine and perfect, but coming down to land at Aberdeen, with the wind and snow, the pilot just couldn't do it, he couldn't land. He shot back up and went round and round trying to land. It was really alarming at this point with all the wind*

and the snow. He said, 'We're really sorry, but we'll have to go back to Edinburgh.' So, we got all the way back to Edinburgh, but he wouldn't let us off the plane. I rang the King to tell him that we are stuck on the plane. We finally got off the plane, and when I rang the King again, he said, 'I really need to see you.' We were stuck in Edinburgh and so Don hired a car. We drove from Edinburgh to Birkhall over the notorious Glenshee Pass. It was a whiteout. You couldn't see the road! You couldn't see the road! You could see nothing! At least if we were stuck in the car, I would be with Don, and he's wise and smart and won't panic. He's from Northumberland and he'll know what to do in snow. Anyway, amazingly he drove, and I don't know how he did it. We got up there at 11.15 p.m., and, bless him, the King was still waiting. He was so worried about us, and insisted that we had to eat. We nibbled at our supper, rather cold and somewhat shocked, and we managed to get all of our business transacted.

Setting Up the Fund

In these conversations, the Prince mentioned on a number of occasions the need to set up a fund to provide grants to support village communities that he feared would simply disappear without financial help. In 2009 at a dinner at Clarence House with Donald and some business leaders, the Prince set up a Rural Action Leadership Team, and from there the idea of a fund gathered pace, driven forward by the Prince himself. In 2010 the Prince's Countryside Fund was set up.

The fund received significant support from the retailer Waitrose. A deal was struck between the Duchy of Cornwall (owned by the Prince) and the retailer whereby the Prince's own brand of biscuit, Duchy Originals, was taken over by Waitrose. In return, profits from the sale of the biscuits were ploughed back into the Fund. Mark Price, Managing Director of Waitrose (who as we saw in chapter seven had invited Donald to manage the board of the Leckford Estate, and in chapter eight was involved with Donald in Food and Farming Futures), became the Chair of the Prince's Countryside Fund, and he very effectively used his influence in the food industry to leverage support from other companies to get the fund up and running. Donald became a trustee of the fund, and he felt that this was a very exciting, challenging development in the support of rural communities.

The fund was open to applications from communities to develop local initiatives. These might include, for example, a training facility for young people, or the establishment of a community shop. Clear guidelines were set out to make it as easy as possible for groups to apply, with criteria laid out so that each bid could be evaluated on its merit.

After the United Kingdom left the European Union, the Prince and the directors wanted to help farmers in navigating the new territory in which they found themselves, and so a new fund was established called the Prince's Farm Resilience Fund. This was to try to ensure that farmers had the right skills and experience to increase output and productivity. The fund was boosted by a million-pound grant from DEFRA. Morrison's, the supermarket chain, were also very generous in supporting the fund. As a result, many hundreds of initiatives were given the financial assistance they needed. The model was so successful that DEFRA copied it and established their own fund to support more initiatives to help farmers prosper outside the European Union. All of this came from the Prince's original vision.

Chair of the Fund

Although never officially Vice-Chair, Donald was occasionally asked to deputise for Mark Price. As Managing Director of Waitrose, Mark had lots of business commitments, and so inevitably could not attend every function where the fund needed to be represented. As a result, Donald often found himself hosting events with the Prince of Wales when Mark was unavailable.

In February 2016 Mark was made a life peer, and so entered the House of Lords as Lord Price of Sturminster Newton, and in April he became a member of the government as Minister of State for Trade. Because he had a ministerial position, he could no longer chair the fund, so he phoned Donald and asked him, if Clarence House approached him, would he be willing to take on the role of Chair. Donald felt that it would be a great privilege to do so, and gladly agreed when he was officially asked.

The Prince of Wales would often make visits to rural areas in different parts of the country, and he expected Donald as Chair to be there with him on these visits. When meeting with farmers, the Prince's concern for their welfare and his knowledge of farming life were very evident, and so his visits were very greatly appreciated. He continued to seek Donald's counsel on policy matters, and Donald was very impressed by his depth of knowledge and understanding of complex issues.

The Prince, with Donald's assistance, had a number of meetings with various interest groups, usually over dinner, to try to influence their practices. For example, they met with major food retailers to try to persuade them to consider amending their pricing policies to help farmers, and also to contribute to the Prince's Countryside Fund. They also met with large landowners to try to persuade them to maintain a structure of family farms to encourage young new entrants into the industry.

One of Donald's responsibilities as Chair was to recommend to Clarence House new trustees to replace those who had retired. One of these new trustees was Heather Hancock, who would take over Donald's position as Chair in 2021. Having been a trustee for eleven years, Donald felt that it was time to retire. He knew that the conversation explaining this to the Prince would not be easy, having worked closely with him for so long. When, however, Donald suggested that Heather Hancock was willing to become Chair, the Prince was very supportive because he knew and trusted Heather. Donald found the situation quite surreal:

> To be suggesting to him, as Prince of Wales, that I should be retiring from this role when he hadn't even started his lifetime's work that he was destined to take on, was very strange.

Donald retired from the Chair in 2021, and Heather took his place. Looking back, Donald was able to say:

When I was growing up and saw the young Prince Charles, who could believe that I would later on have a close working relationship with the future King? It's absolutely incredible.

Charles acceded to the throne in September 2022. It no longer seemed appropriate to call the fund the Prince's Countryside Fund, and so it was renamed the Royal Countryside Fund. Nevertheless, his contribution to farming support over decades was recognised by *Farmers' Weekly* in 2021 when he was given the honour of the newspaper's Lifetime Achievement Award.[74]

74. 'Farmers' Weekly Awards 2020: Lifetime Achievement Award' (*Farmers' Weekly*, 8th February 2021).

CHAPTER TWELVE

Supporting Farmers Through Crisis

The 1990s' Farming Crises

As we saw in chapter five, Donald began his work with the MLC at a time when the industry was faced with major crises, particularly associated with livestock disease, which had a devastating effect on the lives of ordinary farmers. It was not just livestock farmers who were affected; the whole of agriculture, including cereal farmers, faced a massive decline in their income, partly through the strength of the pound. Donald described the 1990s as '*a decade of unparalleled and dramatic change for the industry*'.

Accountants Deloitte & Touche published a report in October 2000 in which they stated that average net farm income had fallen by ninety per cent between 1995 and 2000. They expanded on that by stating, '*That means an average 200-hectare family farm, which five years ago earned £80,000, must now survive on little more than £8,000.*'[75]

---

75. 'Rural landscape under threat as Deloitte & Touche reveals lowest ever returns' (*Deloitte & Touche News,* 12th October 2000).

Ben Gill, President of the National Farmers' Union, stated in response:

> *The public has witnessed the devastation of trade and businesses in this country's pig sector and the pressures facing our dairy farmers. These figures now demonstrate that our arable farmers are also on the rocks.*[76]

This fall in farm income meant that many farming families struggled to make ends meet. In addition, many faced the emotional impact of having to destroy their livestock as a result of measures taken to control the disease that afflicted their herds. Some farmers simply could not cope, and so tragically ended up taking their own lives. In 2001, inquests were held in the Welsh county of Powys into the deaths of three farmers who, according to a newspaper report *'killed themselves because they could not cope with the pressures of their crisis-stricken business'.* The report went on to quote the coroner, Councillor John Hollis, who said, *'The crisis in the farming industry has been catastrophic for the families of these three decent men and their deaths are to be deeply regretted.'*[77]

The government did try to provide help to the industry through various schemes, such as the agri-monetary system, that aimed to compensate farmers for changes in the exchange rate, or through compensation for the slaughter of animals to prevent the spread of disease. Inevitably this was not enough for many farmers, including those who unfortunately felt forced to take their own lives.

---

76. 'Average farm incomes to go into the red next year, report shows' (*NFU Press Release*, 12th October 2000).
77. 'Farming suicides blamed on crisis' (*The Guardian*, 15th June 2001).

In addition to government assistance, there were charities that tried to provide a lifeline to farming families who were in distress.

The main farming help charities that were in existence at the beginning of the new millennium in England were as follows:

1. The Royal Agricultural Benevolent Institution (RABI) currently has King Charles as Patron and the Duke of Gloucester as its President, and a royal charter to govern its work. At its core it believes that no member of the farming community should have to face adversity alone, and they aim to provide counselling support, mental-health training, financial support and practical advice.

2. The Farming Community Network (FCN) has a large network of volunteers across the country who are available sixteen hours a day to provide support to farmers who need advice and counselling. It has a Christian core, having been set up as a joint venture between the Agricultural Christian Fellowship and the Arthur Rank Centre that supports rural communities and churches. The network currently estimates that over six thousand people a year benefit from their support.

3. A newer charity is the Addington Fund, which was set up in 2001 in the wake of the disastrous effects of swine fever and foot-and-mouth disease. It gives emergency help through, for example, the provision of cheap rental housing when farming families most need it, starter homes for young people beginning

their careers in the farming industry, and emergency animal feed for those farmers who could not afford to buy any.

A lot of good work was carried out by these charities, but government officials felt that if the charities were able to work in partnership, their work would be more effective and the government would be more able to support them. And that is where Donald came in.

The Farming Help Partnership

Baron Henry Plumb (formerly President of the NFU and President of the European Parliament) was a patron of the RABI. He knew Donald well, and so in 2010 he approached Donald saying that these charities needed to be working more closely. He asked Donald if he would call a meeting of representatives of the charities. Donald called together the trustees of the charities to discuss the possibility of forming a partnership to support one another.

Donald realised when he met with them that the work they were doing was complementary, in the sense that they were not competing with each other, or getting in each other's way. They were not, however, working together in raising funds, or passing on clients to one of the other charities that could perhaps support them better. What Donald was suggesting to them was that they should provide more of a holistic service to support members of the farming community who were in need. As a result, they formed what they called the Farming Help Partnership and by 2012 they had agreed, with Donald's guidance, a

Memorandum of Understanding that would guide them in their partnership work. The memorandum listed a number of objectives to help members of the farming community, but top of the list was *'presenting a joined-up service and avoiding duplication of effort and confusion of roles to potential clients and donors'*.

Other bodies came on board to join the partnership. Forage Aid, which was formed in 2013 by Andrew Ward to provide forage for farm animals during times of flooding or drought, joined the partnership, providing not only expertise but access to haulage to transport forage and bedding.

Donald also established a link between the Prince's Countryside Fund and the charities. The Prince saw these charities as a good barometer of the state of farming, and so his fund was able to have better intelligence as to where to target farming support. Donald was also able to use his influence, assisted by the support of Elizabeth Buchanan, a trustee of the Prince's Countryside Fund, to help the charities lobby DEFRA to provide greater support, through, for example, the speeding up of subsidy payments to farmers at times of difficulty.

Donald was instrumental in setting up the partnership and he has continued to encourage its development. He is Vice-President of the RABI, and he has regular meetings with the FCN and the Addington Fund. These are not simply 'talking shops' as Donald will always cut to the chase in discussions to ensure that families receive the help they need in times of distress.

In addition, because Donald was known as a committed Christian, he was occasionally asked to preach at services run by the charities. The Addington Fund invited him to preach twice at their harvest thanksgiving services, and on one occasion Prince Charles and Camilla were in the congregation. The FCN also invited him to preach at a service in Ripon Cathedral.

These different charities were prepared to come together as a partnership under Donald's guidance because of the utmost respect they have for him. His close friend, Gordon Gatward, who helped to establish the Addington Fund, when he was Director of the Arthur Rank Centre, had this to say about Donald's involvement:

> *It was because Don was so respected as a Christian, an agriculturist, a diplomat and a politician that he managed to draw them together and enable them to work very closely together.*

Through giving practical help to these charities and by preaching God's Word, Donald was able to share God's love with the farming community when they most needed it. This was recognised by the RABI in October 2024 when he was presented with a Lifetime Achievement Award for his work with farming charities.

CHAPTER THIRTEEN

Social Farms and Gardens

Care Farming

In 2003 Donald's friend and Director of the Arthur Rank Centre, Gordon Gatward, whom we mentioned in the previous chapter, was approached by a number of people who wanted to set up a care farm. Gordon had to confess that he did not know anything about care farms, and so he set about investigating. He discovered that there were a number of care farms across the country. These farms aimed to use agriculture and the countryside as a means of therapy for people who were going through all sorts of problems, with the aim of trying to restore their health and provide rehabilitation. Gordon drew a group together and then convened a national conference that was attended by approximately two hundred and fifty people who were already involved in, or were interested in, becoming involved in care farming. It was clear from the conference that the delegates wanted a network through which they could support each other. From there, the National Care Farming Initiative was set up, later to become Care Farming UK, and was chaired by Gordon.

Gordon was keen to get Donald involved in the charity, and Donald was certainly excited at the prospect. He was very encouraged that those with learning disabilities (people who were close to his heart, given his experience with Jane) were finding a sense of achievement in working with animals, and that those with mental-health problems were finding peace in the countryside. He was impressed that farmers were taking inmates from prisons and training them in agricultural work. Likewise, there was much scope to use farming and the countryside to help young people who were struggling in a conventional school setting, either because of their mental-health problems or the behaviour issues they manifested when in school.

Donald supported Gordon's work, and he was able to use his influence to create a link between care farming and government departments and agencies. He encouraged them to apply for funding from the NFU Mutual Charitable Trust to provide financial support. According to Gordon, *'he was always there in the background'*. He was also there to support individuals who wanted to get involved with care farming. One such person was John Purves.

Happy Hens

John is Donald's brother-in-law, married to his sister Sheena. For most of his life he had been managing the long-established family funeral business, William Purves, Funeral Directors, and which he latterly ran. He also has a degree in agriculture from Edinburgh University. His interest in agriculture was probably sparked by spending his summer holidays on the Curry family farm at Low

Burradon as a teenager, sitting on the mudguard of a tractor next to Donald as he was turning hay, *'holding on for dear life'.*

After graduating, John worked at Kirkley Hall College of Agriculture in Northumberland, but then went back to Scotland to work in the funeral business, which he took over after his father died. He still longed to be involved in farming, and so when the opportunity came to sell their house in Edinburgh and buy a farm in Peebles-shire, John and Sheena jumped at it.

As both the funeral business and the farm developed, John and Sheena felt increasingly challenged as Christians as to what they should be doing with their resources. They had read a newspaper article about a scheme run by Roger Hoskins, a Christian farmer in Derbyshire who took on to his farm challenging young people who were finding difficulty remaining in school. Roger gave them opportunities to work with his poultry. They decided to go down and see Roger, who told them, *'The only qualification that you need to do this is you have to love unlovable people.'*

John and Sheena felt called to do something similar on their farm, and so in 2009 they set up a free-range hen house for twelve thousand hens. They contacted the local secondary schools and got their grateful support to provide work experience for some of their most difficult students. A team of volunteers came together from different local churches, led by a retired Christian IT specialist called Bob White who worked on the farm. It was very much a Christian endeavour with a team who had a vision to help these troubled young people. One local teacher even cut her hours at school to come to help with the project. Each group of young people came to the farm one day a week for the whole year, with a different group coming each day of the week. They tended to come with various problems that affected their behaviour and their school attendance. Initially many of them came to the farm very reluctantly, and showed in their behaviour and attitudes that they did not really want to be there. Soon, however, they began to enjoy working on the 'Happy Hens' project, looking after the poultry, collecting eggs and doing all the work that was required of them on the farm. This included keeping meticulous records of how much feed was given to the hens and the number of eggs produced. These young people who had not taken well to academic work, found that their skills in numeracy and literacy improved as they carried out practical tasks with the hens. Of course they also learned the discipline of work, which would be so important to them in their future lives.

The young people and the volunteers spent their break times together in a Portakabin based on the farm. Meals and snacks were all taken together. The young people eventually relaxed with the adults and opened up to them about the issues in their lives. Some of the boys, for example, were from single-parent families and were very resentful towards the men that their mothers brought into their homes. Bob, in particular, tended to have a very good relationship with the young people, and he always made himself available to listen to them. Over the course of the year many of the young people changed markedly, and some eventually found employment in agriculture.

John and Sheena found it a joy to meet with other Christians who were involved in the project. The volunteers came from a number of different denominations and professional backgrounds, as well as spanning a wide age range, but they were all united in their mission to help these young people. They formed the 'Happy Hens Community' and often met together on Sunday for lunch and to pray for the young people.

Donald had taken a keen interest in the project from John and Sheena's initial thoughts and encouraged them to go ahead, giving them advice where he could. Care Farming England and Wales had been going for some time, and Donald wanted to look at the possibility of establishing Care Farming Scotland. In 2009 he convened a meeting in the Scottish government offices in Edinburgh, attended by government officials and representatives of other bodies, including the prison service. John attended the meeting, although no other farmers did. From that meeting, Care Farming Scotland was born.

Social Farms and Gardens

John and Sheena continued with their 'Happy Hens' project until 2019, by which time they had reached the age of seventy, and it was also when Bob wanted to retire. It seemed the right time to bring the project to a close. They found it increasingly difficult to source funding for the project, as Care Farming Scotland was not a large enough charity to raise money for the different schemes running in Scotland. It became part of Care Farming UK, and that itself widened its remit to join with other charities, for example those running city farms, to form Social Farms and Gardens. The charity, as did Care Farming before it, seeks to use farms, gardens and the countryside to help people with their social and mental problems.

Donald is very active in Social Farms and Gardens, and indeed he is currently President of the charity. He meets at least twice a year with the charity's officials to hear their concerns and provide advice. He is also able to use his political network to arrange meetings with ministers and government officials across the Department of Health, the Department of Education and DEFRA to promote the work of the charity. Sophie, Duchess of Edinburgh, is the charity's Patron, and Donald has found her to be very supportive, encouraging and enthusiastic.

Donald, however, was not only interested in charity work within the United Kingdom; he also had a passion for Africa, as we shall see in the next chapter.

CHAPTER FOURTEEN

Anglican International Development

South Sudan

The world's newest sovereign state to be created is a landlocked country in East Africa, officially called the Republic of South Sudan. After what seemed like interminable decades of civil war in Sudan, South Sudan finally became independent on 9th July 2011. What looked like a fresh new beginning for this fledgling state, however, turned into a nightmare as the country descended into a civil war in 2013 that lasted seven years, and from which it is still trying to recover.

Simon Tustin, the current Executive Officer with Anglican International Development (AID), describes the country's problems using the terms 'Conflict, Corruption and Climate Change'. Conflict has been ever present in the lives of the members of this nation as tribal groups attack each other with hateful violence, all vying for power. Living in a culture of fear of death and destruction means that families cannot settle to grow crops and earn a living. This has created a major refugee crisis for the country that has also spread into neighbouring countries. The United Nations Refugee Agency (UNHCR) estimated in July 2023 that 2.3 million South Sudanese people were internally displaced within the country, and that another 2.4 million have been displaced as refugees to other countries. These are massive numbers, and tragically sixty-five per cent of all South Sudanese refugees are children.[78]

Corruption is another major blight on the country. Transparency International has produced a Corruption Perceptions Index measuring the perceived level of corruption in each of the world's nations. A country that is 'very clean' receives a score of one hundred, whereas a completely corrupt country would be given a score of zero. South Sudan was given a score of eight in 2024, making it the most corrupt nation in the world.[79] Although there may be some subjectivity in these figures, the scale of the problem is rife: corruption is rampant in government institutions, courts, businesses and, sadly, parts of the church. Inevitably, the people who suffer most as a result of this corruption are the poorest, most vulnerable members of society.

The other major problem affecting the country, according to Simon Tustin, is climate change. This has brought severe flooding, and once more the poorest members of society suffer. The United Nations International Children's Emergency Fund (UNICEF) reported in October 2021:

78.   www.unhcr.org (accessed 16.7.24).
79.   https://www.transparency.org/en/cpi/2024 (accessed 31.7.25).

South Sudan is suffering increasingly from the consequences of climate change. A compounded three years of severe flooding has left two thirds of the affected areas facing some of the highest levels of malnutrition. It is common to see families displaced by floods using a tarp to float down the Sobat River in search of higher ground. They pack what they can, which is not much. This is also dangerous for them as they are in the intense sun, they lack food, could be robbed, could run into crocodiles and snakes or be overturned by hippopotami.[80]

As a result of conflict, corruption and climate change, South Sudan is an exceptionally poor country suffering a high degree of malnutrition, poor infrastructure and low levels of educational provision and attainment, bringing it to the bottom of international rankings of Gross Domestic Product. As such, it was a country that needed much help from the international community, including the Christian community.

In 2008 the Global Anglican Futures Conference (GAFCON) held a conference in Jerusalem with delegates representing the conservative wing of the Anglican Communion. They were concerned that many churches within the communion, including the Church of England, were drifting away from biblical truths. The conference produced the Jerusalem Declaration, setting out the statement of faith that the Anglican Communion should be upholding. Also at the conference, some African bishops pleaded

---

80.   Lisa Lynn Hill, 'Climate change leaves the upper corridor of South Sudan flooded out and stuck in the mud' (UNICEF, October 2021).

for help in dealing with the dire situation in what would become South Sudan.

One of the delegates at the conference, David Holloway, vicar of Jesmond Parish Church in Newcastle upon Tyne, had had experience of working in Sudan before he started training for the ministry and he knew what a turbulent country it was. He, along with others, responded to the African bishops' call in 2008 by forming a new charity, Anglican International Development (AID), to support relief work, economic development and Christian ministry in South Sudan and surrounding areas.[81]

Transforming Lives in Africa for Now and Eternity

That is the strapline for AID, clearly summarising what it aims to do. Given the appalling conditions in South Sudan that we have just described, there is much to be done to transform people's lives. For example, despite being a very fertile country, people are suffering from the effects of malnutrition, and so AID has established small agricultural projects, alongside local leaders. This enables families to provide for themselves and earn incomes from their produce. Water, sanitation and hygiene (WASH) is a critical issue, and AID provides help to communities to follow the rules of hygiene, to build and use toilets in the home, to treat unclean water in their homes, and to help to provide, repair and maintain boreholes as a long-term source of water. There is a shortage of health workers, and so AID has established a programme of

---

81. For more detail on David Holloway's experience in the Sudan, please refer to Jim Cockburn, *Contending for Truth*, pp. 158-161.

training local midwives and clinical workers at the Jonglei Health Sciences Institute. Microfinance projects have been established whereby small loans are given to people (mainly women) who want to become part of a scheme to start their own businesses. Those involved receive training and support, and are expected to repay their loans at a low rate of interest once the business is up and running.

All of these projects are built on a Christian foundation, and so, for example, a meeting of a microfinance group would begin with Bible study to learn more about God, and prayer to thank him for his provision and the opportunities he has given them to improve their lives. With the work centred upon God, the hope is that lives would not only be transformed now, but also transformed into eternity as people come to a living faith in the Lord Jesus Christ. In education, AID supports the Wings Academy in Kenya, which has a Christian foundation, giving the students not just academic skills for life, but an understanding of biblical truth that will point to a faith in Jesus.

Although there are lots of churches in South Sudan, the pastors often lack depth in their theological understanding, and so find it hard to help church members grow in their faith. AID is involved in theological training by supporting Bishop Gwynne School of Theology in Juba, the capital of South Sudan, and in particular by sponsoring students from that school to attend the world-renowned George Whitefield College in South Africa to receive in-depth theological training, and then to come back to lecture at Bishop Gwynne School.

Although it may be said that AID is barely scratching the surface in South Sudan (and surrounding countries such as Kenya and Uganda), lives have nevertheless been transformed both now and for eternity.

Donald as a Trustee of AID

Donald and Rhoda had started going regularly to Jesmond Parish Church about three years before the formation of AID. David Holloway realised that Donald was a wise businessman with a depth of knowledge about agriculture and with utmost Christian integrity. As such, he would be an ideal person to join the board of AID, and so David asked him to become a trustee. Donald believed that God was calling him to use his gifts and experience in this way and so accepted David's invitation. As he explained in an interview recorded for the AID website:

I have a deep concern for Africa, having been a number of times, and seen the immense challenges there are in Africa. It was God's timing, not mine, that led to David approaching me to be involved in AID. It came at a moment when it felt right that I should accept this request, particularly to be involved in a Christian, biblically based charity that wanted to work with the church and try and reach communities through that infrastructure of the church in South Sudan. That's what really appealed to me, not just any secular charity, but a charity that was determined to try and deliver a Christian response to the many challenges that are faced in South Sudan.[82]

In his role as a trustee, as well as attending regular board meetings to oversee the work of the charity, he made two visits to South Sudan, the first in 2011 and the second in 2014. These visits gave him first-hand insight into the problems faced by local communities and how AID field workers are able to use their expertise to work with local people to improve their standard of living. Donald and other trustees got the chance to meet with government ministers and officials, the British ambassador, bishops and the Archbishop of South Sudan. These were key people of influence, whom AID needed to work alongside in partnership. The Episcopal Church of Sudan was of particular importance, not only to spread the gospel and to see Christian growth, but simply from a practical point of view to reach people to get them involved in projects. The church was the only real infrastructure there was in large parts of the country, and the only channel through which they could communicate with people.

Donald and his colleagues oversaw the establishment of the microfinance programme, Manna Microfinances, in the capital Juba. Those who wanted to start their own businesses were recruited through the churches, and were given small loans to get their enterprises off the ground. Through these enterprises, the producers and traders were able to support their families and have enough money to pay for their children to go to school. They were committed as Christian people to repaying their loans (plus a low

---

82. https://www.anglicaninternationaldevelopment.org/an-interview-with-lord-donald-curry/ (accessed 25/7/24).

interest payment), even when circumstances were more difficult for them. Donald was encouraged by the Bible study and prayer that took place at the beginning of the weekly repayment meetings, where it was evident that they were trusting God for their businesses and families. Sadly, it was only women who were involved, as the men were more interested in carrying guns and discussing politics than being involved in community businesses. Work was left to the women of the community.[83]

Donald was also able to see progress made with sanitation programmes, particularly in the overcrowded parts of Juba where people had fled during the civil war. This included small things such as encouraging hygiene in the home through washing their hands, to larger projects such as digging latrines and wells. Fresh supplies of water meant that the people did not have to drink polluted water from the Nile. Donald was particularly excited that cholera as a communicable disease was becoming less virulent:

Thousands of lives are saved by doing these simple things. We were really pleased that in the areas we were working in, we reduced the incidence of cholera significantly, just because people were adopting more hygienic practices.

Donald's key interest, of course, was agriculture, and he tried to establish agricultural programmes so that farming communities could be encouraged to become more productive. When he met with the Minister for Agriculture, Donald asked him what percentage of the

---

83. Donald believes that this is still pretty much the case in Juba today, although microfinance projects established by AID in Kenya do have men involved.

country's foodstuffs they were growing themselves. He was shocked when he was told that it was probably only seven per cent, with the rest made up by food imports. Donald is quoted on the AID website saying:

The potential in South Sudan for growing its own food, for developing its agriculture, is huge. And it's so frustrating that in a fertile country like South Sudan, with the Nile running through it – it has some of the most fertile land in Africa – and yet because of conflict, because of civil war, because of tribal disruption, they grow very little of their own food. They suffer from famine and so there is a huge challenge and a huge opportunity to help South Sudan grow its own food.[84]

As was AID's policy, Donald worked with local church leaders on setting up agricultural projects. Some godly leaders were very helpful, but unfortunately not all church leaders were trustworthy or financially competent, and Donald got his fingers burned over one project. In this case, a local pastor was working with displaced refugees in a camp. He seemed to be a godly man, but he was in danger of burning himself out trying to support so many needy people. He decided that he would like to buy a small plot of land to house a mill to crush grain for the people to eat. Donald and his colleagues felt that the pastor had presented his case well and that this was a worthwhile project. AID provided the funding on condition that the capital was paid back over a three-year period. The project started off well and repayments were initially made on time. Unfortunately, they gradually took longer to come

---

84. https://www.anglicaninternationaldevelopment.org/our-work/agriculture/ (accessed 25.7.24).

through and eventually they stopped altogether. This pastor had the best of intentions, but he did not have good financial oversight, failed to carry out any auditing, and got himself into a financial mess.

Donald learned from this case that the due diligence processes carried out had to be more robust before starting new projects. It was agreed, for example, that before granting any financial requests, site visits had to take place, and that AID workers had to be completely satisfied that they could rely on the integrity and financial competence of those involved.

Church services in South Sudan tended to be long and lively. Donald attended one church service where there were 2,850 people in the church. The service started at nine o'clock in the morning and Donald finally left at one o'clock in the afternoon. Communion took two hours to administer to such a large congregation.

The preacher, in his sermon that morning, likened the people of South Sudan to the children of Israel in the Old Testament. As it is recorded in Exodus 16, when they were in the wilderness the Israelites were fed by the Lord who provided daily portions of bread (manna), enough to satisfy their needs. When the people crossed the Jordan into the Promised Land, they had to cultivate the land for themselves. The preacher drew out the parallel for the people of South Sudan that at one time they had to rely on handouts from relief agencies, whereas now they had to learn to cultivate the land productively for themselves. That epitomised Donald's philosophy in working with AID;

the farmers needed to be taught new, productive methods rather than giving the people handouts.

Despite evidence of corruption in parts of the church, Donald was encouraged by the commitment of many Christians that he met. When he saw the conditions in which they lived, and their simple faith, relying on God, he found it *'inspiring and it really got under his skin'.* He was greatly impressed by the faith of one particular Christian that he met, a lady called Eunice. She believed that God wanted her to build a hotel in which people could come and stay. She had no money but she prayed and prayed. As a result, through the generosity of others, God provided her first of all with a piece of land, and then tents for people to stay in. Later she was given resources to build a canteen, and then building materials for bedrooms. She employed local women to work with her on the project. She had prayed constantly and saw the Lord's provision. When she told Donald her story, he asked her what she was praying for now, and she told him that she was praying for a hospital. Donald felt *'just blown away by this woman's faith'.*

The Unique Qualities Donald Brought to AID

As we have seen in previous chapters, Donald leaves his own individual imprint on any organisation that he serves, and the same has been true in his role as a trustee of AID. Simon Tustin, AID's Executive Officer, has come to know Donald very well and has developed a very high regard for his wisdom and judgement since he took on his role in 2020. Indeed, Donald actually interviewed Simon for the post on behalf of the trustees in 2019 at a session in Portcullis House in Westminster. (Donald was by then a member of the House of Lords, and so could use parliamentary facilities.)

Simon realises that Donald loves Africa and wants to see lives transformed now and for eternity, in line with AID's mission statement. He is seen as a man of faith who knows the grace of God, but he is no soft touch and, as Simon says, *'he holds my feet to the fire'* by asking questions such as, *'Have you checked?'*, *'Where is the business plan?'* or *'How is this going to be funded?'* Simon sees Donald as *'a good example of someone who is business minded and godly and understands the grace of God and how God provides, but he doesn't allow me to be slack'*. Donald wants correct procedures to be followed and due diligence to be done, particularly given the high level of corruption in South Sudan and so many opportunities for things to go wrong.

One example of this that Simon was able to share was when he wanted to provide additional support to the people of Minga, who had to flee when their community was attacked and their houses set on fire in April 2024. Almost seven thousand people were internally displaced to Rokon where they settled with the support of Bishop Emmanuel, the local bishop. This was a terrible, but sadly not uncommon, tragedy in South Sudan. The situation got much worse once the rainy season started, and it was clear that the community needed more help.

Strictly speaking, AID is not an emergency relief organisation, but Simon wanted to respond to this need by sending more money than was originally budgeted in order to construct boreholes and latrines. Simon knew that Rev.

Jonathan Pryke, Chair of the board, would not authorise the spending unless Donald felt that the project was viable, and so he emailed both of them with his business case. Donald asked for further information, including what other options there were, and what the opportunity cost was in terms of AID's other commitments. This was Donald holding Simon to task. Once he knew that Donald was satisfied, Jonathan authorised the spending.

Donald chairs the agricultural development group, a group of godly experts that he has been able to pull together. Simon has seen Donald's skill in chairing meetings at first hand, a skill that we have seen others commenting on in previous chapters:

Everyone knows that he is very good at dealing with people, which he is, but he cuts to the chase in a very clear and calm way, and keeps things simple wherever possible.

Donald ensures that the meetings of the group are absolutely focused, with the meetings beginning with a Bible passage and prayer and lasting a maximum forty minutes. The group asks Simon practical questions, which he admits he had not thought about, such as whether he has planned for sufficient storage for crops to prevent them from being eaten by rats or destroyed by rain.

Donald also brings his political expertise to the board. Again Simon comments on his political skills:

He knows how politics works. He knows what politicians are like, and he is able to work in that environment in a godly way, accepting all the limitations of people and

the system and still operate as a faithful, godly, wise
Christian. He is a realist, but not a cynic.

As a member of the House of Lords, he is able to use his influence there to garner more support for AID amongst politicians. For example, he has spoken in debates on South Sudan, explaining to his colleagues how difficult life is there for people trying to scrape a living in the midst of civil war. He has hosted lunches in the Lords to which about twenty politicians attend, and where he and Simon can present the agricultural issues facing AID. He has a large network of contacts, and Simon has been able to tap into these contacts.

AID's funding can be quite precarious, and so it is important to '*keep pedalling*' as Simon would put it, by embarking on new projects, generating good news stories and gathering in more prayer and financial support. Donald understands that, and he has played an important part in bringing in additional funding through his contacts.

Donald's unique approach to serving the Lord through the work of AID has been as committed and professional as his approach to his other charity work and his decades of service in domestic agriculture. He longs for more lives to be transformed in Africa now and for eternity.

PART FOUR

Serving the Lord in the Lords

CHAPTER FIFTEEN

Becoming a Peer of the Realm

So Why Not Go Into Politics?

That was a question that Donald was constantly asked after he had taken on high-profile government roles. After all, he had caught the public's attention during the BSE crisis as Chair of the MLC, he had headed up the Policy Commission on the Future of Farming and Food, he had been an 'honorary minister' in the implementation of the recommendations of the Policy Commission, and he had chaired the Better Regulation Executive. This farming lad from rural Northumberland had achieved so much and in such unexpected ways, as he operated in the highest echelons of government. Of course, Donald knew that it was God who had been working through him as he took on these roles, and it was God who had worked things out for his purposes. He knew as David did as he wrote Psalm 16:

> I say to the LORD, 'You are my Lord; apart from you I have no good thing.'[85]

---

85. Psalm 16:2

But the question was still there, '*So why not go into politics?*' He knew that he definitely did not want to become a Member of Parliament; he had never asked anyone in his whole life to vote for him and he was not going to start now. Also, like his old friend Ben Gill who had been asked the same question, he would not know which party to stand for. He had spent all of his public life deliberately being politically neutral, and he had shown no interest in party politics.

There was another problem stemming from the way that he had been brought up. Growing up in the Brethren movement, he had been taught that those who belonged to Jesus should believe that '*our citizenship is in heaven. And we eagerly await a Saviour from there, the Lord Jesus Christ, who, by the power that enables him to bring everything under his control, will transform our lowly bodies so that they will be like his glorious body*'.[86] Donald firmly believed that. He knew that being a citizen of the heavenly kingdom was of greater value than any earthly citizenship, and that one day Jesus would come back from heaven and gather all of his people to be with him.

There was, however, part of the Brethren teaching that he was much less sure about: the teaching that because the world was sinful, Christian people should not be involved in its administrations. Donald felt that this went against the stewardship commission that God had given Adam and Eve in the Garden of Eden:

---

86. Philippians 3:20-21

God blessed them and said to them, 'Be fruitful and increase in number; fill the earth and subdue it. Rule over the fish in the sea and the birds in the sky and over every living creature that moves on the ground.'[87]

As Donald wrestled with these conflicting thoughts, he finally decided that although his citizenship was certainly in heaven, nonetheless, it was his responsibility '*to do good works, which God prepared in advance for [him] to do*'.[88] If God wanted him to go into politics, he was prepared to do just that.

Some people planted thoughts in his mind about becoming a member of the House of Lords, if he felt uncomfortable about becoming a Member of Parliament. There was the possibility of becoming a cross-bench peer, which did not require any party allegiance. In 2010 he and Rhoda began to pray earnestly about it, and it did seem that there was a recurring answer that he should consider applying to become a life peer. Therefore, he completed the online form and sent it off, leaving the whole matter in God's hand.

He heard nothing for months, and so assumed that God did not want him to go down this path after all. Then out of the blue he got a letter from the House of Lords Appointments Commission, inviting him for interview. He duly turned up at the House, where he was interviewed by a panel chaired by Lord Michael Jay, formerly British Ambassador to France, and who had invited Donald, when he was MLC Chair, to events at the British Embassy in Paris. Seeing a familiar face put Donald at his ease, but nevertheless it

---

87. Genesis 1:28
88. Ephesians 2:10 ('*us*' in the verse changed to '*him*' to apply directly to Donald)

was a fairly rigorous process, where Donald had to talk about what expertise he would bring to the Lords, what his special interests were, and how much time he could give to the role. He must have satisfied the panel because a couple of months later he received a phone call from Michael Jay, saying that they would like to appoint him, subject to the approval of Downing Street and Buckingham Palace. So on 13th October 2011, he was created a crossbench life peer taking the title Baron Curry of Kirkharle. He thus began his life as a peer of the realm in the House of Lords.

Life in the Lords

After his appointment had been formalised, Donald started his induction into the Lords with a tour of the building and detailed explanations of how things worked. He found it all rather overwhelming, as he recalled:

> *At the end of the tour, I think that I will have to do this all again two or three times before I become familiar with the layout of it all, as it had just become one big blur of an ancient building with all the history associated with it. It was all rather mind blowing. The staff were all very helpful, and I was given a mountain of books to read to explain the procedures, the protocols, and how the political process worked.*

On 13th October 2011 he was formally introduced into the Lords, following the traditional centuries-old procedure when he had to swear an oath of allegiance to the Queen. He donned ermine robes, and was supported in the swearing-in process by two supporters, who both had an agricultural background, Lord Henry Plumb (a former NFU President) and Baroness Hazel Byford (a farmer from Leicestershire and a Conservative agricultural spokeswoman). His choice of supporters reflected Donald's own interests, but on reflection he wonders if he made a mistake choosing two Conservative peers; he was an independent peer, and people may have thought that he was a 'closet Tory'! Nevertheless, it was a grand occasion with peers shouting 'Hear, Hear' at the end of the ritual after Donald had shaken the Speaker's hand. Rhoda and members of the family were present in the gallery, and they thoroughly enjoyed it.

During his first few months in the Lords he was able to use his time wisely, getting to grips with parliamentary procedures and protocols, and getting to know his parliamentary colleagues. He shared an office with Lord Singh, the first Sikh member of the Lords, who was introduced to the Lords on the same day as Donald. Although they were clearly from different faith backgrounds, they shared much in common on moral issues, such as gay marriage and abortion. He also began to make good Christian friends in both the Lords and the Commons.

An important part of his work in the Lords was participating in committees and reviewing legislation that had passed through the Commons and was now making its way through the Lords. The crossbench group of peers wanted to be sure that his agricultural expertise was well used, and so he was often appointed to committees associated with agriculture and horticulture. Later on in 2020 when the Agriculture Bill went through the Lords, the crossbench peers were very happy for Donald to take a lead on certain aspects of the Bill, and he guided them through the process.

It was not only on committees related to agriculture that Donald sat, but also on other issues, such as energy and the environment, industrial regulation (using his experience from the Better Regulation Executive) and even the serving of refreshments in the Lords (which was important to Donald as he saw the value of hosting meals in the Lords for various organisations, such as potential supporters of AID). Donald believed that it was important for his Christian witness to try to gain respect across the Lords by being involved in a range of issues, otherwise he would not have influence when it came to debating specifically Christian, moral issues. God gave him success in this, as he is highly respected across the political spectrum in the Lords.

Donald had to wait a few months before he was able to make his maiden speech in the Lords, but finally, on 6th February 2012, he spoke in a debate in the Moses Room when the Grand Committee debated a report from the European Union Committee on agricultural innovation. This particular debate was an ideal opportunity for Donald to introduce himself and give some of his views on the state of agriculture in the world.

He began his speech by sharing how honoured he was to be welcomed into the Lords, and he paid tribute to his supporting peers, Lord Plumb and Baroness Byford. Indeed he said, '*The noble Baroness is, I am thankful to say, still rescuing me when I get lost or step out of line.*' As Baron of Kirkharle he gave some of the history of the estate, including gory details about a previous baron, Robert Loraine, who was '*barbarously murdered by the Scots in 1483, returning home from the church where he had been at his devotions*'.

He went on to talk about the subject of the report, and he endorsed the need for greater innovation to deal with the great global imbalance between those who are obese as a result of eating too much, and those who are suffering from malnutrition. He also expressed concern at the environmental impact of much agricultural production and how scientific research had to be exploited to reduce greenhouse gas emissions. In his conclusion, he emphasised the role of the next generation:

> *We need to invest in schoolchildren so that they have an understanding of these issues, and we need to invest in career development opportunities so that we attract young people who can help deliver the sustainable systems necessary – whether they be scientists, teachers or technicians who want to work in agriculture because it is such a fascinating challenge, and an exciting opportunity at such a pivotal point in history.*[89]

The Value of the Lords

For large numbers of people the House of Lords is an anachronism, belonging to some other time in the distant past, dominated by pomp and ceremony, and undemocratically populated by members who do not relate to the general population of the United Kingdom, and are only there as a result of privilege and patronage. The newly elected Labour government is committed to reforming the House of Lords and ultimately replacing it

---

89. Lords Hansard (UK Parliament, 6th February 2012) https://hansard.parliament.uk/ Lords/2012-02-06/debates/12020638000251/details#contribution-12020638000044 (accessed 31.7.25).

with an alternative second chamber. As the first of these reforms, it introduced a Bill in 2024 to remove hereditary peers from the Lords, and at the time of writing it is about to be passed by both parliamentary houses.

Donald firmly believes that reform of the Lords is necessary, but he also passionately believes that it has a vital role to play in our constitutional processes as a revising chamber, able to scrutinise the often poorly drafted legislation that is sent to it from the Commons. He made his views clear in the debate on House of Lords reform in December 2024.

In that debate, he expressed that the plan to remove hereditary peers was *'vindictive'* and *'an attack on privilege'*, and that by so doing the Lords would lose hardworking members who *'put in a real stint'*. He suggested that there are *'dozens of peers who never turn up and do not contribute to the working of the House – so why not sack them as a first step?'*[90] He had no objection to an age limit being established or a limit on the length of term of office, for as he said, *'It is an immense privilege to be here, but none of us is immortal and I would support a fifteen-year term.'*

Perhaps his real concern, as expressed in the debate, was that the legislation had been *'generated in an immature House of Commons that has very limited knowledge about the role of this House and how it functions.'* In other words, he felt that the proposals were flawed and piecemeal, as they were produced by a new government, supported by members, many of whom were new to Parliament and

---

90. His colleague, the Earl of Lindsay, who is himself a hereditary peer would largely agree with Donald's view, but would qualify it, saying that there are some peers who are not very regular attenders, but who are very influential when they come because of the particular expertise that they have.

lacking the experience and wisdom necessary to make a major constitutional change.

He wanted the Lords to be proactive in suggesting change. *'We in the Lords should be bold and brave in proposing reforms for the Government to consider.'* Towards the end of his speech, he gave some suggestions for reforms, including reducing the power of Prime Ministers to appoint members to the Lords, and instead giving the Appointments Committee the responsibility of appointing members, ensuring *'political balance, professional balance, diversity balance and geographic balance'.* He proposed either an age limit or a limit on the term of office (or both). Minimum attendance and participation requirements should be established. If hereditary peerages were to be abolished, then at least current hereditary peers should be allowed to continue in the Lords until they reach whatever age limit or term of office limit is introduced.[91]

It is that tone of speech that has won Donald respect in the Lords. Rather than simply being negative about a piece of government legislation, he wanted to put forward proposals that would make the Lords work more effectively as a revising chamber. That is in the nature of Donald's character that we have seen again and again in his work with different organisations.

In the next chapter we shall look at some of the debates to which Donald contributed in the Lords.

---

91. Lords Hansard (UK Parliament, 12th November 2024) https://hansard.parliament.uk/Lords/2024-11-12/debates/83328063-65F9-4679-B470-836D454464B9/details#contribution-A9C8ED00-E579-4A52-99DD-8FC4DF3585B1 (accessed 31.7.25).

CHAPTER SIXTEEN

Debating in the Lords

Offering Socks to Peers

During his time in the Lords since 2011, Donald has made a large number of contributions to debates. He knew that he was there for a purpose, and so he was not one of those peers who rarely turned up to the House, or who remained silent during debates. As we indicated in the previous chapter, he spoke on a wide range of topics, so that he was not seen as a narrow-minded Christian farmer, only interested in debates of a religious nature or those concerning agriculture. He had a lot of experience in different fields that he could bring to the debating chamber. If he gained respect as a result of speaking on a range of topics, he believed that people might listen with greater interest to what he had to say about the gospel of Christ.

During each debate he spoke clearly, making his points with authority, but also where appropriate with humour. He would have a speech prepared on his iPad, but he was not afraid of deviating from it. He was able to refer to the contributions of previous speakers, either to endorse them or to disagree with them (albeit gently and with good humour). For example, in his very first debate in the Lords' Chamber on the Scotland Bill in 2012, when the issue of the appointment of a Scottish Crown Estate Commissioner came up, he was able to set the record straight about the current rigour of the appointment process. Speaking from his own experience as a Crown Estate Commissioner, he said:

I was actively involved when commissioners from England, Scotland or Wales were appointed to the board of the Crown Estate and can assure noble Lords that it takes the process of appointment very seriously indeed.[92]

Likewise, when Assisted Dying was debated in 2021, Lord Vinson, a supporter of the motion, claimed that Christ was helped in his death '*by a kindly Roman centurion, who pierced his side with a sword*'. Donald had to correct Lord Vinson's theology by stating at the end of his speech:

We live in an imperfect, fallen world. Support for this Bill will not make it perfect. In closing, I challenge the interpretation of theology given by the noble Lord, Lord Vinson. Christ's death was not assisted. He voluntarily offered up his life and it was the purpose for which he came.[93]

92. Lords Hansard (UK Parliament, 28th February 2012) https://hansard.parliament.uk/Lords/2012-02-28/debates/12022860000567/details#contribution-12022860000095 (accessed 31.7.25).
93. Lords Hansard (UK Parliament, 22nd October 2021) https://hansard.parliament.uk/Lords/2021-10-22/debates/11143CAF-BC66-4C60-B782-38B5D9F42810/details#contribution-428665F1-B7D6-4291-A99F-09C7CFC1F546 (accessed 31.7.25).

Donald could, of course, have made his point even more strongly by stating that it was not the centurion who pierced Jesus's side, but that it was one of the soldiers (and not a particularly kindly one at that), who pierced his side *after* he had died.[94] Donald did not want to humiliate completely the noble Lord who claimed to be a Christian for his lack of biblical knowledge.

He was also able to 'ad lib' humorous comments in his speeches. In a debate in 2020, when Donald was pushing for the government to extend the High Speed rail line further north, he began by making light-hearted comments on his colleague Lord Adonis's tie:

My Lords, it is a privilege to follow the noble Lord, Lord Adonis, whose commitment to HS2 is very well known. I must say that I am impressed with his tie. I have a pair of socks which I clearly need to donate to him to match.[95]

In his speeches, he tried to attack the topic from a unique angle, so that it would not simply be a repetition of what others had said before him. It is clear from his contributions that he had done his homework and that he knew his material very well. Although he had his speech in front of him on his iPad, he did not really need his notes because they were well embedded in his mind. This is something that we have already seen in his work with a variety of organisations such as the NFU and the MLC.

94. John 19:30-35
95. Lords Hansard (UK Parliament, 30th November 2020) https://hansard.parliament.uk/Lords/2020-11-30/debates/F87429A2-85A7-42CC-AE17-F3B1FA17F891/details#contribution-8FDC9AE8-AFA7-4446-B93B-76B06A240C85 (accessed 31.7.25).

He worked hard to research the issues associated with each topic that was being debated. He was assisted in this by his CARE graduate mentee, who would ensure that he was fully briefed for debates. Donald would often give his mentee the framework of what he wanted to say and ask the mentee to put the detail in. He then made amendments so that it would come across in his own style. We shall look more closely at the CARE Leadership Programme in the next chapter.

He also received advice from external bodies, including the Christian Institute, a Christian charity based in Newcastle. The Institute has been able to keep Donald up to date on upcoming issues of concern to Christians. Simon Calvert, Deputy Director of the Christian Institute, as a keen observer of events in Parliament, had this to say about Donald:

> As a Christian, he speaks out faithfully, wisely and graciously on some of the most challenging issues. He shows significant courage, and is often one of the first to speak out. He is uncompromising on points of principle, whilst showing a real understanding of where people are coming from, and so showing an ability to communicate and reach out to people who are not naturally in sympathy with his position. By the demonstration in public and in private of Christian character, he has managed to maintain the respect and affection of many people who wouldn't agree with him.

In the rest of the chapter, we shall examine some of the many contributions that Donald has made to debates.

As we do so, we shall group them under the headings of: Agriculture, South Sudan, Human Rights and Moral Issues.

Agriculture

We mentioned in the previous chapter that the crossbench group of peers wanted to ensure that Donald's agricultural expertise was well used in the House, either in the work of committees or in full debates. During his time in the Lords, he spoke on a number of issues related to agriculture.

In June 2021, for example, he spoke on the recently published Food Poverty Report, calling on the government to procure local food for schools, hospitals and other public bodies, decrying the dependence on food banks, praising the work of Christians Against Poverty, and asking the government to ensure that education about the importance of food is embedded in the curriculum.[96]

Later that month he spoke in the Environment Bill debate, and emphasised the need for soil quality regulation, saying (based on his work with the Lawes Trust):

The degrading of soil is a worldwide problem with huge consequences for the natural environment. As a soil scientist at Rothamsted Research told me many years ago, once soil has been completely degraded, it cannot be recreated. Its loss can be permanent, with all the consequences that might lead to.[97]

96. Lords Hansard (UK Parliament, 10th June 2021) https://hansard.parliament. uk/Lords/2021-06-10/debates/DC98F4E1-85F9-4C9F-BF99-00DCE5CE2787/ details#contribution-C7666E28-7417-4B93-A47E-C69FA5BF45EE (accessed 31.7.25).
97. Lords Hansard (UK Parliament, 21st June 2021) https://hansard.parliament. uk/Lords/2021-06-21/debates/81AD12F2-8FBB-41AB-BD5B-0000F1218177/ details#contribution-DA3DFEEF-551B-4B2F-BBD5-0A9421C5485A (accessed 31.7.25).

He spoke on horticulture in October 2022, using his experience of the establishment of TIAH. He asked the government to promote the development of skills in the industry, invest in science (alluding to the forthcoming breakfast launch of the paper that he had co-written 'Application of Science to Realise the Potential of the Agricultural Transition', as mentioned in chapter eight), and invest in new technology such as robotics.[98]

There are, however, two areas of debate related to agriculture that need more attention: the Agriculture Bill that went through the Lords in 2020, and the controversy hitting the farming community at the time of writing, that of the removal of the exemption of inheritance tax on agricultural property.

Let us look at some of Donald's numerous contributions to the debate on the **Agriculture Bill**. In his first speech on the Bill, he declared its importance and how much he welcomed it:

Much has been said already about the significance of this Bill: to take a blank sheet of paper and have the opportunity to shape how our countryside is going to be managed for the next two, three or four decades is a huge privilege and an immense responsibility. The Bill must be fit for purpose. The direction of travel as outlined in it is absolutely correct.

He went on to declare the Bill's potential benefits to establish a sustainable food programme within the context

---

98. Lords Hansard (UK Parliament, 13th October 2022) https://hansard.parliament.uk/Lords/2022-10-13/debates/367A6370-1EB3-4223-8AFF-F37304AB5BFE/details#contribution-EFB2EBAC-399A-48F2-9AED-44AA598EC300 (accessed 31.7.25).

of strong environmental management of the countryside. He was, however, concerned with deficiencies within the legislation. For example, he felt that following Brexit, trade deals were being negotiated that could well result in cheap food imports that were not subject to sufficiently rigorous standards. Also, he felt that the timetable was too short, as farmers were not yet ready for the change from direct support of their output to assistance based on the Environmental Land Management Scheme. He put it very strongly:

> *The scale of the change is unparalleled and time is short. Farmers need advice and time to make correct decisions about their future. We are not ready.*[99]

In a further debate on the Bill in July, Donald moved an amendment to include developing an understanding among children of the value of farming, food and diet, as well as an understanding of the environment, to be included as part of farmers' commitment to the public good for which they would receive payment.[100]

Part of the discussion during the Bill's journey through the Lords was whether food security should be considered a public good, rather than simply a private good. If it were a private good, farmers would only receive the market price for their produce. If it were a public good, however, and thus of benefit to society as a whole, farmers should receive more than simply the market price to ensure that

---

99. Lords Hansard (UK Parliament, 10th June 2020) https://hansard.parliament.uk/Lords/2020-06-10/debates/EC829DFD-0FAF-4DCA-94DE-9431DBB2A966/details#contribution-C8660739-08A5-4A14-BFF3-224BAA6A3907 (accessed 31.7.25).
100. Lords Hansard (UK Parliament, 9th July 2020) https://hansard.parliament.uk/Lords/2020-07-09/debates/0F2A8115-10FC-4BB6-A4EE-D3AC12DFC9B8/details#contribution-44E60286-63F3-4359-BF8E-5710C3209293 (accessed 31.7.25).

there was an adequate supply of food at a time of national crisis. A few days later Donald tried to get the Minister, Lord Gardiner, to agree that food security was indeed a public good and whether it should not be seen as such in preparation for a potential national food crisis:

I suggest to the Minister that it may be appropriate to reconsider whether food security should be included as a public good, should the Government need to intervene at some stage in future.

Lord Gardiner was not, however, willing to agree to Donald's request.[101]

Later in the month, in a further day of debate on the Bill, Donald made a number of contributions. He reiterated his concern that the gap between the support farmers receive under the current payment scheme and what they can expect to receive in 2024 under the Environmental Land Management Scheme will be too large, and that farmers are not ready for such a change. He expressed it very dramatically:

Tens of thousands of family farmers are not prepared for the scale of the change that the Bill will introduce. It is the most fundamental change in support, and the greatest cultural change, that any farmer in Britain today has ever faced. At present, there is no way farmers can prepare for this change because, for obvious reasons, there is no information available

---

101. Lords Hansard (UK Parliament, 14th July 2020) https://hansard.parliament. uk/Lords/2020-07-14/debates/3C546AE8-944B-426B-B85D-B45F99F7FD3E/ details#contribution-3C3BD941-9FA7-40F0-981B-7FDC23345CFA (accessed 31.7.25).

on the basis of which they can begin to consider their future plans and make decisions.

He reassured the Minister that he was '*enthusiastic about this bold change in policy*', but he felt that '*it would be a disaster if such an important change in policy was rushed through and we failed to engage appropriately*'.

In the same debate, he also shared his concern about the proposed frequency of collecting data on food security. The Bill proposed collecting data every five years, and other peers suggested three years. For Donald, even three years was too long to wait. He believed '*that an annual report would reduce the risk of distortion by a global event and clearly identify trends*'.[102]

As the debate resumed after the summer recess, Donald again emphasised the need to bridge the gap in support to farmers, the need to provide transparency in what the support to farmers is likely to look like, and the necessity of not rushing the process of transition.[103]

In a further day of debating, Donald moved an amendment to give the newly established Trade and Agriculture Commission an ongoing role in monitoring standards of traded goods, rather than simply providing one initial report:

My challenge is, why, having established that resource, would one send them all home for Christmas, never

---

102.   Lords Hansard (UK Parliament, 21st July 2020) https://hansard.parliament.uk/Lords/2020-07-21/debates/1F989BDF-5F50-4DE1-B034-D2CDD5488F50/details#contribution-2E5B5F3B-C298-4418-8FB7-EBB570FDB168 (accessed 31.7.25).

103.   Lords Hansard (UK Parliament, 15th September 2020) https://hansard.parliament.uk/Lords/2020-09-15/debates/6CA68B21-0327-495E-AF9B-718248E84E64/details#contribution-ECE2BA46-85E0-4780-9C6B-F7973E4FACED (accessed 31.7.25).

to be seen again? The logic of retaining that valuable knowledge – that talent – to scrutinise future trade deals to make sure that they comply with the standards and terms in their initial report is obvious. I am disappointed that the Government have resisted the pressure to give the commission an ongoing role.

Donald's amendment to give enhanced powers to this new commission was supported during the debate by many peers, who often referred to Donald's eloquence and clarity in presenting his case. The amendment passed by one hundred and seven votes.[104]

In a day of debate in October, Donald emphasised the momentous importance of the Bill in the agricultural history of the nation, likening it to the Repeal of the Corn Laws in 1846 and the Agriculture Act of 1947. He said:

It represents fundamental change: a once-in-a-lifetime opportunity to reshape the management of the countryside and how we redesign our agriculture.

He went on to declare that he believed that his colleagues in the Lords had put forward amendments that had significantly improved the Bill.

To be able to interrogate this Bill line by line and scrutinise with vast knowledge of the subject does demonstrate, once again, the value of this House.[105]

---

104. Lords Hansard (UK Parliament, 22nd September 2020) https://hansard.parliament. uk/Lords/2020-09-22/debates/1A030753-AD32-4AEA-A626-93299698C2EC/ details#contribution-A022970A-E0CC-4839-BA22-A76BAA44887B (accessed 31.7.25).
105. Lords Hansard (UK Parliament, 1st October 2020) https://hansard.parliament. uk/Lords/2020-10-01/debates/FB2BE9C7-E618-4243-8023-2DB177ED0E52/ details#contribution-E70A74E0-EDE5-49D4-9B9F-BEC6BA632814 (accessed 31.7.25).

In the final debate on this Bill, the Minister, Lord Gardiner, thanked peers for their amendments and contributions after what he reckoned was a total of ninety hours of debate. He promised that the government would be taking the issues that had been raised seriously and that most of their amendments would be incorporated in the final legislation. Donald was one of those singled out for particular praise by the Minister.[106]

Another area of debate worth looking at in more detail is the Chancellor's proposals to remove **agricultural inheritance tax exemptions**. We saw in chapter six that 2024 started with farmers' protests over their treatment by government that were disrupting towns and cities, particularly in London and Kent, and also across much of Europe. The year ended and 2025 began with similar disruptive protests from farmers, although this time they were more widespread across the United Kingdom and it was a purely British issue; farmers were furious at the changes proposed by Chancellor Rachel Reeves in her November 2024 Budget, over changes to exemptions on death duties on agricultural property.

In order to raise revenue, the Chancellor proposed from April 2026 to reduce very significantly the Agricultural Property Relief that has been available to farmers before they were eligible to pay death duties on their land. Relief was to be capped at a million pounds. This may seem a large amount of relief that farmers will still receive, but farmers and peers in the Lords supporting them, argue that farms

---

106.   Lords Hansard (UK Parliament, 9th November 2020) https://hansard.parliament.
       uk/Lords/2020-11-09/debates/2348B191-9F1B-4BA2-BBCC-DBADFF75B7A5/
       details#contribution-FA3AADFF-DC42-4588-B5F5-0D0385D48C54 (accessed 31.7.25).

do not generate sufficient profits to pay the inheritance tax that would be due under the Chancellor's proposals on the death of the farmer.

The Earl of Leicester opened a debate asking the Lords to note the effect that these measures would have on small farms and family businesses. He called the budget proposals *'structural vandalism of the farming ecosystem by a Government that did not consult, did not listen, did not learn and did not see the flaws in their plan'.*

Donald took part in the debate, making his points with his usual passion and clarity. He showed his empathy for farmers who already faced serious financial difficulties that would only be made worse by the proposed changes to inheritance tax:

Until six years ago I was a tenant farmer, having started farming in 1971 with very little capital. I mention this because I know what it is like to be under serious financial pressure. I can relate to those thousands of family farms – farmers who are worried, stressed and unsure about the future of their businesses. I know what it is like to lie awake at night knowing that there is not enough cash to pay the bills, having difficult conversations with the bank manager when the overdraft limit is exceeded, having to arrange extended credit and having lots of hire-purchase agreements.

He reiterated a number of the difficulties faced by farmers brought about by changes in government policy that he has shared in previous debates, particularly the complex transition to the new Environmental Land Management Scheme. He stated forcefully the opposition to the

Chancellor's proposals on inheritance tax exemptions for farmers:

> *Against this background, the Budget decision on inheritance tax has been the final straw. I applaud the Chancellor on achieving a remarkable feat. She has succeeded in completely uniting the entire farming sector.*

Part of the government's argument is that relatively few farming businesses will be adversely affected each year, perhaps as few as five hundred. Donald pointed out, however, that the effect needs to be considered over a generation. He quoted estimates from the Central Association of Agricultural Valuers, which suggest that 75,000 businesses would be affected over a generation; their ability to pass the family farm on from one generation to the next would be severely limited, something that is *'potentially devastating for farming families'.*

He gave a moving example of the possible effects on one family:

> *A lady spoke to me after the demonstration a couple of weeks ago. Her aunt, who is eighty-six, asked whether she thought the Assisted Dying Bill[107] would be in place next year, because she needs to die next year before the changes to inheritance tax take place. Otherwise, her family will have to sell the farm.*

---

107. The aunt was referring to the Leadbetter Bill that was going through the Commons at this time. This would be a case of an elderly lady feeling under pressure to go through with assisted suicide as a solution to deal with a family's potential financial difficulty brought about by changes to death duty exemptions.

Almost all of the peers who spoke in the debate were, like Donald, opposed to the Chancellor's proposed changes. Lord Livermore, the Financial Secretary to the Treasury, although understanding the depth of feeling in the chamber, believed, however, that the measures were necessary, given the state of the public finances and the need for consistency across all sectors of the economy.[108]

South Sudan

As we saw in chapter fourteen, Donald is passionate about Africa and he is very concerned about the plight of the poverty-stricken people of war-torn South Sudan. He has used his position in the Lords not so much to promote the work of AID, which he always registers as an interest in any debate on the topic, but to continue to make the outside world aware of the traumas suffered by the people, and to encourage governments to take stronger action in support of the country. In this, he has been well supported by other peers who were concerned about the human tragedy developing in a country that had held out so much promise.

In his first speech on the subject in a Grand Committee debate in 2012, he spoke of the need to diversify the economy and reduce its dependence on oil and foreign aid. He emphasised the importance of the church, as it was the only institution capable of reaching the people to promote healthcare and food programmes. He lamented the fact

---

108. Lords Hansard (UK Parliament, 12th December 2024) https://hansard.parliament. uk/Lords/2024-12-12/debates/10C84930-3837-4B94-8BDC-141283B57661/ details#contribution-5EA82ACD-5C9E-444C-AC5B-043F907D9F9C (accessed 31.7.25).

that a country that could be *'part of the bread basket of Africa'* was only five per cent self-sufficient in food. He called upon the British government to develop links with the government of South Sudan as it is *'an emerging democracy that is going to need significant help'.*[109]

Donald was to speak again a few months later on the subject in a debate on the European Report on Sudan and South Sudan. This was just three weeks after he had visited the country, and so his impressions were very much fresh in his mind. He spoke again about the importance of the church in the country, and the need for good governance and a justice system that was free from corruption. He and other speakers were concerned about the lack of co-ordination of non-governmental organisations and aid agencies that were *'falling over themselves in their desire to help'.* He ended his speech by saying:

> *South Sudan is a high priority. We must not relax our efforts to assist and to help to influence the transition from civil war to independence, to stable and sound governance with good healthcare and education facilities and economic stability. I hope that our Government will seriously address these issues. We have a huge responsibility.*[110]

Six years later, he tabled a question that began a debate on South Sudan:

---

109. Lords Hansard (UK Parliament, 26th March 2012) https://hansard.parliament.uk/ Lords/2012-03-26/debates/1203271000130/details#contribution-1203271000063 (accessed 3.8.25).
110. Lords Hansard (UK Parliament, 17th October 2012) https://hansard.parliament.uk/ Lords/2012-10-17/debates/12101783000320/details#contribution-12101783000177 (accessed 3/8/25).

To ask Her Majesty's Government what steps they are taking to address the current humanitarian crisis in South Sudan and to support the delivery of a lasting peace settlement and longer-term economic and social development.

In his speech he outlined the horrors the country faced as a result of the civil war prompted by the rivalry between President Salva Kiir and his Deputy, Riek Machar, *'warmongers with big egos, who are prepared to sacrifice vast numbers of their own people to try to gain control'*. He spoke about the intensity of the refugee problem and the economic calamities that the country faced as a result. As such, it was very difficult for the country to attract investors, as they regard the situation as being so unstable that it would simply be *'pouring millions of dollars down the drain'*. As in previous speeches, he spoke of the church as *'one of the very few routes available to connect with local communities'*.

He told the House of the need to intensify efforts to promote and enforce a ceasefire, and to train leaders for the future from young people across tribal divisions, as he sensed that they were embarrassed about the state of their country and wanted to do something about it. He finished his speech with a challenge that he had been given by Eunice, the lady to whom we were introduced in chapter fourteen: *'You will come back, won't you? So many people never come back!'* In essence, he was asking our government not to give up their support for South Sudan and people like Eunice.

Other peers congratulated Donald for tabling his question and securing the debate, and made speeches in support of increased government action to help the people of South Sudan. Finally, at the end of the debate, Lord Burt, Minister of State at the Department of International Development, gave this promise on behalf of the Government:

In answer to the challenge about South Sudan, we will not walk by on the other side when people are suffering. That is not what the UK does. That is our reputation in this world. We will not give up hope.[111]

Human Rights

Donald was clearly concerned about human rights in South Sudan, but he also cared deeply about human rights abuses both in this country and beyond. This included the rights of people to have a faith and live out their beliefs, freely expressing their deeply held convictions.

Early on in his parliamentary career, he made a speech in the chamber about **the importance of religion in British society** and the dangers that it faced from a growing secularism. For him, the United Kingdom was definitely not a secular state, and so, for example, the monarch makes vows to God during the coronation service. He believed that the influence of Christianity made our society much more tolerant. He felt, however, that the atmosphere in the public square was changing, and that Christians felt increasingly ignored and their work despised. It was harder for Christian charities to obtain funding. He quoted

---

111.   Lords Hansard (UK Parliament, 4th July 2018) https://hansard.parliament.uk/Lords/2018-07-04/debates/E0DDD10E-5940-4CDA-ABAB-CF3841F558A8/details#contribution-789E1410-2673-4A01-9C97-56080D7A520E (accessed 3/8/25).

the example of a Baptist homeless charity that was told that it would lose its funding because it allowed people to say grace before meals. Another example was the case of Brighton Council threatening to remove funding from Pilgrim Homes, because they refused to insist that their elderly residents completed a questionnaire on their sexuality.

He was concerned that the country would have to follow the *'we don't do God'* ideology expressed by Tony Blair's press secretary, Alastair Campbell. He finished his speech by saying:

> *The power of God can change lives and influence communities and society. It has done so in the past. Doing God and doing good is what millions of people in Britain want the freedom to do today.*[112]

In March 2024, during Holy Week, Donald took part in a debate on **the global persecution of Christians**, with those taking part consistently decrying the physical and emotional persecution of Christians in countries by members of other faiths or by autocratic governments who saw no place for the Christian faith in their countries. Two months before, many of the peers had attended a presentation in Westminster by Open Doors, a ministry supporting persecuted Christians. The statistics presented in their World Watch List were shocking, with, for example, an estimated total of 365 million Christians suffering high levels of persecution for their faith. These statistics were used by peers, including Donald, in their speeches.

---

112. Lords Hansard (UK Parliament, 22nd November 2012) https://hansard.parliament. uk/Lords/2012-11-22/debates/12112245000890/ details#contribution-12112245000531 (accessed 3/8/25).

Donald admitted in his speech that throughout its history the church itself was often guilty of persecuting members of other faiths and indulging in ethnic cleansing, actions that were completely at odds with the teaching of Jesus in the parable of the Good Samaritan. The situation faced by persecuted Christians today, however, is intolerable, *'because the data suggests that more Christians are being persecuted today than at any time in our history, and the number is increasing daily'.* He cited the cases of Nigeria and India, with both countries seeing an upsurge in violent attacks on Christians.

These cases are often neglected in the world press, where attention is more focused on Gaza and Ukraine. Donald, however, wanted our government to take a lead in standing up for the persecuted church. For that to be effective, there first of all needed to be an awareness of the fear that many Christians in this country have of *'recrimination, of losing their jobs, of being alienated and ostracised, or cancelled, to use today's ridiculous jargon'.* He finished his speech by saying:

> *We need to stand firm to defend our Christian freedoms, our ability to promote the Christian gospel. We cannot claim to be a global exemplar if freedom of speech is under threat here. The very thing that we are concerned about globally is at risk in Britain. We must not tolerate intolerance of our freedom to practise Christian faith and values here at home.*[113]

---

113. Lords Hansard (UK Parliament, 25th March 2024) https://hansard.parliament. uk/Lords/2024-03-25/debates/CB6143EE-0EAF-4202-9167-7F1D96B4F5E9/ details#contribution-2A3DBA8B-A68D-4D99-AD60-23C8A726270C (accessed 3.8.25).

In 2020 Donald took part in a debate on the **Trade Bill**, which he described as *'a critically important bill'* in light of Britain's departure from the European Union. He and other colleagues wanted to be sure that the newly established Trade and Agriculture Commission properly scrutinised the establishment of free trade agreements with other countries. The Christian peer Lord Alton wanted to ensure that the protection of human rights was part of that scrutiny process, and so he moved an amendment to the Bill, that in essence said that the United Kingdom should not participate in any trade agreement with any state that had committed genocide.

Donald strongly supported that amendment, demonstrating the hypocrisy of making trade deals with countries involved in genocide:

We absolutely cannot condone genocide and must, through the channels available to us, uncover and condemn it. To condemn genocide on one hand as a nation state, and then be willing to negotiate trade deals and perpetuate trading arrangements is inconsistent in the extreme. It would be hypocritical, and the Government would be guilty of turning a blind eye to atrocities that have been proven to be taking place. Walking past on the other side, to use a biblical phrase, is not a stance that a responsible global state should adopt, and it would undermine our moral influence.[114]

---

114. Lords Hansard (UK Parliament, 7th December 2020) https://hansard.parliament. uk/Lords/2020-12-07/debates/5D794716-8635-4759-9739-2DCD263F86DE/ details#contribution-CEB11B1F-ACED-449B-BB5E-03E23B09DCE9 (accessed 3.8.25).

Domestic abuse was another area of concern for Donald, including the abuse of people with disabilities. In May 2021, Baroness Campbell introduced an amendment to the **Domestic Abuse Bill** that would widen the scope of those who would be protected by the Bill to include those with disabilities who were maltreated by their carers. Donald supported this amendment and spoke of his concern for such people, citing his experience of looking after Jane and running At Home in the Community. He argued that those in care are in particular danger of abuse as their sometimes-challenging behaviour can lead to tempers being frayed, and their inability to communicate can mean that abusive behaviour can continue for a long time before it is detected.

Unfortunately Baroness Williams, the Minister in the Lords responsible for the Bill, did not agree, as she felt that it would widen the Bill too much. Baroness Campbell, however, was determined to put her amendment to a vote, with the result that her amendment was passed with a majority of eighty-four votes.[115]

Donald took part in another day of debate on this Bill later in the month. The subject this time related to the smacking of children, following an amendment moved by Baroness Bennett that would remove the justification of smacking on the ground that it constituted reasonable punishment. Donald spoke out strongly against the amendment, as he felt that reasonable chastisement was enshrined in law to protect parents who were not in fact child abusers, but

---

115. Lords Hansard (UK Parliament, 8th March 2021) https://hansard.parliament. uk/Lords/2021-03-08/debates/340A2BF5-B7C1-4F3E-91B6-48C31AB93791/ details#contribution-681EA5F9-B88C-4C9E-A4B5-106382D6AE5D (accessed 3.8.25).

who were loving parents acting in the best interests of their children. He argued that the existing law protected children in that anything more than a transient red mark on the skin was seen by the Crown Prosecution Service as unreasonable chastisement, which could lead to the prosecution of parents. Opinion polls have shown that the majority of respondents do not want to see loving parents fall foul of the law as a result of giving a child a tap on the hand or a smack on the bottom. He summed up his arguments by saying:

> *There would be a real danger in including this amendment in the Domestic Abuse Bill. Loving parents are not domestic abusers and it is insulting to suggest otherwise. A gentle tap on the hand to discourage a persistent two-year-old from putting their finger in every plug socket they encounter is not child abuse but responsible parenting. Abusive parents are already caught by the law, but this amendment would task police and social services with targeting not abusive but loving parents. It would be a serious mistake.*[116]

Baroness Bennett decided not to call for a vote on this amendment, withdrawing her amendment accordingly.

Moral Issues

Donald spoke on a number of occasions on matters related to sexual ethics or on the sanctity of life. For example, early

---

116. Lords Hansard (UK Parliament, 15th March 2021) https://hansard.parliament. uk/Lords/2021-03-15/debates/2DB5363F-1D41-4E5A-B2E2-3CA3A2D5A28B/ details#contribution-E87060E1-3BCB-47FE-8AE3-B737B05A646C (accessed 3.8.25).

on in his parliamentary career he took part in the **Marriage (Same-Sex Couples) Bill**. This was a Bill that Prime Minister David Cameron was pushing through Parliament in 2013, legislation that he later proclaimed gave him great pride and that he hoped to export throughout the world.[117]

Donald certainly did not share the Prime Minister's enthusiasm; he felt that this redefinition of marriage went completely against his Christian beliefs. It really made him wonder what he was doing there in the Lords. Yet he still believed that God had put him there for a purpose, and that God wanted him to stay there.

He did speak on two areas of the Bill. Firstly, he proposed an amendment to clarify the procedures necessary if a church wished to hold same-sex marriages. He was concerned that there would be divisions within churches with some activists (perhaps a minority) who wanted to push ahead with same-sex marriages and others wanting to hold a more conservative line. He declared:

> *Some churches with no clearly defined governing body – and I know many that fall into that category – will find it exceedingly difficult if a minority decides to pursue this. It has the potential to divide church congregations and communities, and that is deeply regrettable.*[118]

No vote was taken on this, but Donald felt assured that his point had been heard. The other area of the Bill on which he

---

117. Christopher Hope, 'David Cameron: "I want to export gay marriage around the world"' (*Daily Telegraph*, 24th July 2013).
118. Lords Hansard (UK Parliament, 19th June 2013) https://hansard.parliament.uk/Lords/2013-06-19/debates/13061997000100/details#contribution-13061997000057 (accessed 4/8/25).

spoke was in relation to the position of teachers in schools who did not believe in same-sex marriage. How were they to respond if pupils were to ask whether they believed that it was right for those of the same sex to marry?

Lord Dear had moved an amendment to protect teachers in this situation, so that they had the right to express their personal views about marriage, and that they did not have to endorse any particular view of marriage. Donald spoke in support of this amendment, asking the government to give further clarification on this issue, given that *'we all have huge respect for the role of teachers and admiration for what they do'*. Lord Dear's amendment was, however, strongly defeated.[119]

Discussion on same-sex marriage and abortion with regard to **Northern Ireland** took place in the Lords in 2018. At that time, because of disagreements amongst the political parties of Northern Ireland, the Assembly was not sitting. The Parliament at Westminster wanted to make both same-sex marriage and abortion legal in the province as they were in the rest of the United Kingdom, and so it had inserted a clause in its Northern Ireland Bill to make them both legal. There was strong argument on both sides of the debate.

Donald very clearly stated where he stood on these issues:

I subscribe to the biblical view that human life is sacred from conception and that marriage is the union of one man and one woman for life.

---

119. Lords Hansard (UK Parliament, 8th July 2013) https://hansard.parliament.uk/ Lords/2013-07-08/debates/13070845000227/details#contribution-13070917000013 (accessed 4/8/25).

He also made it clear that it was not the place of Westminster to impose its views on the people of Northern Ireland; that was the role of the devolved Assembly in Belfast. Indeed, that Assembly had within the past two years voted against allowing these practices to be legalised. As Donald declared:

> *We must give proper respect to the people, politicians and institutions of Northern Ireland and leave these matters to them.*[120]

These measures, however, became law in Northern Ireland through the enactment of this Bill.

When the Lords came to debate the regulations enforcing **Relationships and Sex Education** in 2019, Donald defended the role of parents to withdraw their children from this part of the curriculum. He had received lots of correspondence from parents expressing their concerns; concerns that seemed to have been ignored in the regulations. He spoke about the '*long-established right for parents to withdraw their children from subjects where there is likely to be teaching that clashes with the views of the family*'. These subjects were religious education and sex education. The right to withdraw the child did not apply to relationships education, although that could well have material with which parents disagreed.

In secondary schools, the headteacher had a power of veto over the withdrawal of children from sex education and so

---

120. Lords Hansard (UK Parliament, 30th October 2018) https://hansard.parliament.uk/Lords/2018-10-30/debates/CE0B2C92-BA77-46CD-A007-F3A2F44566E3/details#contribution-CDBA4C55-BEC6-4685-83B4-6FADFC1FC438 (accessed 4/8/2025).

could overrule the wishes of parents. Even though other peers tried to assure him that this power would be rarely used, he stated that he could not find these assurances in the regulations, which '*unequivocally give the headteacher the final say*'.

As in the debate on same-sex marriage, he was concerned about the rights of teachers who for reasons of faith could not in all conscience teach the RSE material.

> *What about teaching staff who have a faith conviction and work in non-faith state schools? We are already aware of the sad case of Kristie Higgs,[121] who was sacked for expressing concerns about a conflict with her Christian convictions. How many more teachers or teaching assistants are going to find themselves in impossible situations?*

The motion to approve the regulations was nevertheless passed.[122]

Donald has a real passion for protecting children from harmful pornographic material, and was frustrated that progress in legislating against companies who promoted such material was so painfully slow. In February 2023 he

---

121. In 2019 Kristie Higgs was removed from her post as a pastoral administrator in a secondary school for gross misconduct. As a Christian mother, she was concerned about the inappropriate sex education material used in the primary school that her children attended (not the secondary school in which she was employed). She posted her views on her private Facebook account, and when her employer became aware of the post, she was dismissed. Supported by Christian Concern and the Christian Legal Centre, she fought her case for six years, and in 2025 (in the week, as it happens, that this chapter was being written), she was exonerated by the ruling of the Court of Appeal. Kristie publicly gave thanks to God for this landmark ruling protecting Christian freedom of speech.
122. Lords Hansard (UK Parliament, 24th April 2019) https://hansard.parliament.uk/Lords/2019-04-24/debates/8F9DC3B0-CD59-4FB5-9F00-1554B50ADEDC/details#contribution-5ABB7DF9-A3D8-4CD2-922B-FAEF55629BAD (accessed 4/8/25).

wrote an article in *The House*, the internal parliamentary magazine. He began by saying:

> *Like many Members of the House of Lords, I am a grandparent. As with most grandfathers, when I see stories on the news of children harmed by social media, I am troubled. When you hear the tragic case of fourteen-year-old Molly Russell, who took her own life after being inundated with self-harm content on social-media, it's hard not to worry whether the youngsters near and dear to us are being served up the same horrific content when they go online.*

He went on to complain about the slow progress of the **Online Safety Bill** through Parliament, and how the protection offered to children in it was far less substantial than was contained in the Digital Economy Act of 2017, even though, '*shockingly, these protections were never brought into force*'.[123]

He got his chance to speak on this subject in the debate on the Online Safety Bill a few months later in May 2023. Donald expressed his strong concern that children and young people could access harmful pornographic material because the regulator Ofcom was not acting quickly or decisively enough to prevent social media companies from promoting harmful material. He felt that there was too much flexibility in the Bill in its present form, and so he proposed amendments to ensure that the regulator acted more quickly for the sake of those young people who were being harmed by social media content.

---

123. Donald Curry, 'The Online Safety Bill needs more robust protections for children – we cannot afford further delay' (*The House*, 3rd February 2023).

Lord Parkinson, the Minister responsible for the Bill in the Lords, did not accept the need for Donald's amendments as he felt that they would '*undermine Ofcom's ability to regulate in a proportionate way and could make Ofcom's enforcement processes unnecessarily punitive and inflexible*'.[124]

A few weeks later, during the continuation of the same Bill, Donald again spoke on the need for Ofcom to work more quickly. He stated that '*when looking at Ofcom's implementation of existing provisions on video-sharing platforms, the overwhelming impression is of a very drawn-out process, with Ofcom failing to hold providers to account*'. There was a sense of righteous frustration when he said:

> *When children are at severe risk, it is not appropriate to wait. Why, for example, should we allow porn sites to continue to host 10 million child sexual abuse videos while Ofcom simply reports that it is continuing to partner with these platforms to get a road map of action together?*

He mentioned his experience with the Better Regulation Executive; when a regulator acted decisively, those subject to regulation become more compliant, which actually makes life less onerous for the regulator. He wanted this to become Ofcom's experience through this Bill. The Minister, however, while accepting Donald's experience, again felt the powers and flexibility given to Ofcom in the Bill were sufficient to provide the necessary regulation.[125]

---

124. Lords Hansard (UK Parliament, 2nd May 2023) https://hansard.parliament.uk/Lords/2023-05-02/debates/78C7231A-3F91-438E-ABCF-21E577D0EB73/details#contribution-36C44B89-37B2-41A7-BF58-4C8E1A8FA02F (accessed 4.8.25).
125. Lords Hansard (UK Parliament, 22nd June 2023) https://hansard.parliament.uk/Lords/2023-06-22/debates/B6855858-F8BF-4296-8D76-14A527A3B3AF/details#contribution-20E4E579-1A1B-4DCB-8F12-4AD2BA946507 (accessed 4.8.25).

At the time of writing, we are expecting the government to present legislation to ban so-called **conversion therapy**, as promised in the Labour Party election manifesto.[126] This measure, if it were to be passed, is seen by Christians as being very dangerous. Although its proponents use the word 'abuse' to describe the activities of those who try to interfere with people's freedom to change their sexuality or their biological sex, others see legislation in this area taking away people's freedom of speech and thought. Loving parents who try to persuade their children not to try to change their gender may be penalised under this law. Teachers, counsellors and church workers who are approached by people who are confused in this area and who are seeking guidance, may be prosecuted if they give guidance contrary to the legislation. Christian ministers may also be subject to prosecution if they preach what is recognised as traditional biblical sexual teaching.

A Bill on this subject was actually introduced into the Lords as a Private Member's Bill by Baroness Burt in February 2024, four months before the General Election. She called for a ban on conversion practices, expressing frustration that Theresa May, the then Prime Minister, promised a Bill five years ago but no Bill had yet been forthcoming. A number of peers gave a wide range of arguments both in support of and against her motion.

Donald presented his views in this debate clearly and boldly. He made it clear to begin with that *'the UK has an array of laws already in force that rightly prohibit genuinely reprehensible behaviour of the kind sometimes identified*

---

126. Change, Labour Party Manifesto 2024, p. 91.

by advocates of new legislation'. Therefore, there was no need to have new legislation to deal with physical abuse, coercion or threats of violence. His fear, however, was that the Bill would lead to the prosecution of those who expressed certain opinions:

> *Could private prayer and casual conversations fall within the present Bill? I fear that they could. We could see innocent people criminalised for everyday conversations – not for brutalising people, not for some violent programme of brainwashing but simply for talking with other people.*

He reminded the House that conversion was at the heart of Christian experience, turning in repentance and faith to follow Jesus, and he used the apostle Paul's conversion as an example:

> *I am rather disturbed to see 'conversion' used in the title of the Bill in such a negative sense. The experience of Saul of Tarsus on the road to Damascus was an amazing, positive experience and has been for millions since … I am an enthusiast for conversion.*

There was an overall feeling that the motion was badly drafted, admitted by Baroness Burt herself, and so the motion was not taken to a vote.[127]

At the time of writing, Kim Leadbeater MP's Private Member's Bill aiming to legalise **assisted suicide** had worked its way through the House of Commons, and was finally

---

127. Lords Hansard (UK Parliament, 9th February 2024) https://hansard.parliament. uk/Lords/2024-02-09/debates/DB690A34-D945-4EDA-9178-DD6357498F45/ details#contribution-C8B3F669-424C-4119-95AC-0CEE6A189064 (accessed 4.8.25).

passed by a very slim majority of twenty-three votes. It has now pass on to the Lords for further scrutiny and debate.

There have been earlier attempts to introduce legislation in support of assisted dying, particularly in the Lords. One such attempt was the Bill proposed in 2021 by Baroness Meacher who explained in her opening speech what her Bill would achieve:

It would give terminally ill, mentally competent people over the age of eighteen the right to choose the manner and timing of their death. To be eligible for an assisted death, two independent doctors would have to confirm that the person requesting assistance had a life expectancy of no more than six months.

There were many speeches presented on both sides of the argument. Donald spoke from the heart against this Bill, using his own experience from looking after Jane. He recalled that Jane died eight years before, when '*she passed from time into eternity*'. Six years before that, however, she suffered from acute pneumonia and was not expected to live, as the doctors could do no more for her. This was obviously distressing for Donald and Rhoda as they sat with her. Donald admitted:

If someone at that time had offered an assisted dying – assisted suicide – option, I firmly believe that in our heightened emotional state, not thinking rationally, we may have been tempted to agree to her premature death. Had we done that, it would have troubled us for the rest of our lives.

What was amazing was that Jane pulled through, and Donald was able to say:

> *It was a long, hard slog, but she enriched our lives for another six years, enjoyed her own life and continued to influence hundreds of people during that time. What a tragedy it would have been had her life been cut short six years too early. That is exactly what will happen if this Bill is supported. There will be a few in the first year and a few hundred in future years who feel that they have become a burden on their families and society and will be killed off prematurely because it will become the simple, easy option.*

He repeated a sentiment that Lord Sheikh had previously stated, '*Doctors are very poor in predicting when people will die.*'[128]

No vote was taken on this Bill.[129]

Donald recalled afterwards how shocked he was that some peers who had a Christian background, including a former Archbishop of Canterbury, spoke in favour of the Bill.

When Kim Leadbeater's Terminally Ill Adults (End of Life) Bill came to be debated in the Lords in September 2025, Donald, along with many other peers, spoke vehemently against it, as he had done in 2021. Again, he emphasised the sanctity of human life, which '*has been enshrined in the*

---

128. Government data quoted in *The Telegraph* on 21st January 2025 suggest that one in five people who are given six months to live are still living three years later. This backs up Donald's and Lord Sheikh's assertions in the debate in 2021.
129. Lords Hansard (UK Parliament, 22nd October 2021) https://hansard.parliament. uk/Lords/2021-10-22/debates/11143CAF-BC66-4C60-B782-38B5D9F42810/ details#contribution-428665F1-B7D6-4291-A99F-09C7CFC1F546 (accessed 4.8.25).

biblical foundation of our laws'. He was concerned that lives would be devalued, as the Bill would result in massive cost-savings for the Treasury and families being able to protect their inheritances. *'There is absolutely no question that the Bill, if passed, will devalue the importance of human life, and economics will become part of the decision-making process.'* He quoted the experience of Canada in this regard.

He ended his speech by declaring:

> *If we support it, we risk diluting our sympathy and concern for the elderly, the frail, the disabled and the depressed, seeing them as a drain on resources when they opt to live at society's expense rather than conform to the new norm and opt to die. The Bill is dangerous and a retrograde step.*

At the end of the two days of debate on the Second Reading of the Bill, it was clear that significantly more peers spoke against the Bill than for it. It was agreed to set up a select committee to scrutinise the Bill in detail, allowing expert witnesses to give evidence to it.[130]

The Impact of Debates in the Lords

Do the debates in the Lords, including the ones that Donald has contributed to over the years, make a difference to the final legislation that enters the statute books? As we have mentioned before, the House of Lords is constitutionally a scrutinising chamber, with

---

130. Lords Hansard (UK Parliament, 19th September 2025)
    https://hansard.parliament.uk/lords/2025-09-19/debates/E9BB0A6B-3259-4F79-82CE-845506281E4F/TerminallyIllAdults(EndOfLife)Bill (accessed 23.9.25).

the task of going through bills line by line to bring about improvements. Amendments are made to Bills, and perhaps with a series of compromises, the majority are accepted by the government of the day. In the debates on the Agriculture Bill in 2020, for example, Donald was finally able to get his amendment accepted that put the Trade and Agricultural Commission on a statutory footing. His amendment, however, to extend the transition period for transferring farmers on to the new Environmental Land Management Scheme, although supported by other peers, was not accepted by the Minister.

There are certain key reasons for the Lords' amendments so often being accepted. One reason is that, unlike in the Commons, there is no guillotine, so that time is taken to scrutinise legislation without it being rushed through. Lord Ewan Cameron, a peer with great experience in farming and rural issues, gave another reason, and that was the tremendous amount of expertise that existed in the Lords. He stated:

Don and I are experts in rural affairs, and so when Don stands up to speak, he is listened to with great respect for his expertise. The House of Lords is a 'house of experts'.

Even when he talks on issues beyond agriculture, Donald is listened to with great respect because he is admired as a man of integrity, despite the fact that people might disagree with his view. Particularly on moral issues such as abortion and same-sex marriage, when Donald has taken an uncompromisingly Christian view, he has been on the losing side of the debate. Nevertheless, he feels that it is important for the Christian view to be aired, so that people might remember that ultimately it is God's laws and standards that should be pre-eminent in our society, and that they should influence the legislation produced by Parliament.

CHAPTER SEVENTEEN

Developing Future Leaders

CARE

In September 1971 around 45,000 Christians gathered together in Trafalgar Square in a public demonstration of their faith and in a denouncement of the increased secularisation and sexual permissiveness of British society. This was followed by a mass rally in Hyde Park with performances from prominent Christian musicians of the time, including Graham Kendrick, Cliff Richard and Dana. American evangelist Arthur Blessitt preached a powerful message, calling people to follow Jesus.

This event was the Nationwide Festival of Light, and was strongly supported by many of the Christian 'celebrities' of the time, including Malcolm Muggeridge, Mary Whitehouse, Lord Longford and Cliff Richard, as well as church leaders across the denominations. The theme song of the festival, 'Light Up the Fire', even reached number thirty-one in the UK pop music charts. After the festival was over, the organisers continued to meet, ultimately forming a trust to carry on campaigning on issues of concern to Christians in the 1970s and '80s. In 1983 the trust was named Christian Action, Research and Education (CARE) and was chaired by Lyndon Bowring.

Over the last forty years CARE has continued to take its place in the public square promoting traditional biblical values. The organisation's vision, according to their website, is *'to see politics renewed and lives transformed'*.[131] This involves applying God's values in formulating a Christian response to the moral issues that are confronting individual Christians, the church and the nation as a whole. As a result, CARE staff have tackled issues such as pornography, abortion, assisted suicide, gambling, transgender and economic inequality. Material is provided for individual Christians and churches so that they can pray about these issues, as well as taking practical action such as lobbying politicians. They also work with politicians by providing them with high-quality research through briefing notes and even drafting speeches for them.

With campaigning issues such as these, it is no surprise that Donald and Rhoda were keen CARE supporters. Indeed, they supported CARE for a number of years before Donald became a member of the Lords. Soon after he entered the House, he met Lyndon and Celia Bowring for lunch, and they talked through the work of CARE and how Christian politicians like Donald could provide practical support. He subsequently had regular update meetings with the Chief Executives, initially Nola Leach and then Ross Hendry. Through these contacts Donald was able to see more

---

131.   https://care.org.uk/ (accessed 24.8.24).

clearly how he could be of greater assistance to the work of CARE in Parliament.

Empowering Future Leaders

One of CARE's key aims is to develop the leaders of the future by raising up a new generation of young people to serve God in positions of responsibility in Parliament, business and the public sector. Encouraging Christians to take a stand for God's values in developing policy in government, in company board meetings, and in education and health settings would be a major step in fulfilling CARE's vision of renewal and transformation.

In 1993 CARE's Leadership Programme was started. Christian graduates were interviewed and appointed as parliamentary interns, supporting the work of members of both the Commons and the Lords. Since then, about four hundred graduates have come through the year-long programme. Graduates tend to be in placement with two members, and they work for them and meet with them for four days a week. The fifth day is devoted to a study programme looking at leadership, core theology and political theology, and where they also have the opportunity to meet with key people in the public square.

Alumni from the programme are full of praise for the unique set of experiences they were able to enjoy through it. Thirty years after the establishment of the programme, CARE published a booklet allowing alumni to share some of their experiences and their reflections on how CARE helped to shape their future careers.[132] Some of the quotes included in the booklet are:

> *I was able to see the system behind the scenes, warts and all . . . it was invaluable for what I went on to do next.*

> *My MP made me feel like I was in his circle of trust, as a member of his team, a friend, and a Christian brother.*

> *The CARE Leadership Programme is one of the most impactful Christian political serving programmes, and I highly recommend and endorse it.*

> *My desire to be connected to a Christian mission with a very significant purpose came in part through CARE.*

Donald became involved as a mentor in the programme in 2015. There was a practical reason for his involvement: by then he realised that he needed administrative support with the large workload that he was facing. More importantly, he realised that the programme gave graduates an introduction to the parliamentary world, preparing them for leadership in their future careers. Training up younger people is part of the philosophy that he has adhered to throughout his working life, going back to his Northumberland tenant farming days when he was able to encourage young men like David Brodie, John Charlton and Edward Ridley to take on farming responsibilities.

He has usually shared a graduate with an MP so that the young person could have experience of life in both the Commons and the Lords. He tries to meet with the

---

132.   https://care.org.uk/uploads/blocks/LP30-11.pdf (accessed 26.8.24).

graduate one day a week to discuss his diary commitments and what needs to be organised for particular events. If he needs to meet with ministers or officials, the graduate makes the appropriate arrangements. If he wants to speak in a forthcoming debate, the graduate will register this with the Parliamentary Office, as well as carrying out research that Donald can use in his speech.

He also tries to give the young person advice for their future. They talk about the graduate's personal circumstances, including any problems that they currently have and their plans for the future. They discuss issues that are facing Christians in Parliament and beyond at the present time. Donald often has a verse from the Bible that may shed light on what they are discussing, and they often have a time of prayer. Donald tries to give spiritual encouragement, and as he says:

It is more than just an employee / employer relationship, as we have our Christian faith, and we are all part of the Body of Christ. It is very encouraging for me to be meeting these young folk who are just on fire for the Lord.

Philippa Taylor is the CARE staff member who has oversight of the Leadership Programme. She is responsible for recruiting graduates on to the programme, allocating them to mentors, monitoring their progress and planning their study programme. She greatly values Donald's input as a mentor. As she puts it:

People who take on the mentoring role, and I am sure that this is very true for Don, see the value of investing in future generations. Don's reason for taking these young people on is to give an opportunity and to invest for the long term. He uses that year to train someone up, to help them, and then is prepared to start all over again. He is really good at spending time with the graduates, seeing them every week. He will in that time have a cup of tea with them in the tearoom in the House of Lords, when he will do work with them and also find out how they are personally. He will be there for more than just a cup of tea, but he will be there as someone they can talk to. He will be there to encourage and help, sitting in a safe place with them, making sure that they are okay. He is just brilliant on that, really brilliant.

She does warn the graduates about Donald:

Don't be deceived. He is incredibly gentle, very kind, a really fabulous, warm, godly man. Underneath he is absolute steel. He has got a past of remarkable achievements that doesn't come from just being nice. Don't be fooled by the exterior – you don't mess with him.

The graduates very much take to Donald and want to work hard for him, knowing that he cares for them and wants to help them. According to Philippa, there is never a negative word said against him. In fact, *'every time his name is mentioned, people just smile and there is always a warm response'.*

Philippa also uses Donald in the graduates' induction programme at the beginning of their course. He talks to the whole group about his own faith journey, his career both in farming and on the national stage, and the ups and downs in his personal life, including Jane's story. This gives the graduates the chance to see the real person beneath the successful peer.

Let us now consider the experience of one of Donald's graduates, Sarai Challis.

Sarai

Sarai has felt called to work in the political arena, but it was of paramount importance for her that her Christian faith would be able to shine through wherever she worked. She believed that the CARE Leadership Programme would provide an almost unrivalled experience of applying her faith within the sphere of politics, and so, having prayed, she applied for a place on the programme. She was called to a selection day when she was interviewed by senior members of the CARE team as well as completing a written exercise, drafting a briefing note and a speech on assisted suicide. As a result she was given a place within the 2022–2023 cohort of CARE graduates, joining eleven others. Sarai believed that this was such a tremendous privilege:

> *There's nothing quite like being with eleven people who you are very aligned with when it comes to what you believe in and value (not necessarily politically!), all starting out in the same career in this place which is so prestigious. Every day you go in you had to pinch yourself a little bit that you are really there. It was an extreme privilege.*

Philippa allocated two mentors to Sarai: Donald and a Christian Conservative MP, Robin Millar, who had a Welsh constituency. Sarai described how she looked up to them both in a CARE publicity video for the Leadership Programme:[133]

It was extremely humbling working for two Christians who hold such impressive positions in their respective spheres. Not only did I get to see Christ modelled in our corridors of power, but I also got to see what it means to serve in a position of leadership.

A strong bond of mutual trust and respect developed early on between Donald and Sarai. Donald spoke to the whole cohort as part of their induction programme, and he recalls Sarai asking at the end, *'And what can we pray for you, Lord Curry?'* When they first met, Sarai saw Donald as being very warm and easy. Working with him, Sarai saw how *'incredibly astute'* he was, and in meetings with ministers and officials he knew his subjects very well and *'he never dropped the ball'.*

Donald helped Sarai get to grips with the challenges of understanding and following parliamentary procedures as she navigated her way across both parliamentary houses. Part of her role was to carry out the administrative work that was necessary to allow Donald to function effectively as a peer, such as managing his diary, arranging for him to meet officials, finding meeting rooms and organising events. She also drafted papers and speeches for him and made sure that he was fully briefed for debates that he was participating in.

133. https://www.youtube.com/watch?v=rvefDVoG7zY (accessed 3/9/24).

When they met each week, he took a very proactive interest in how she was getting on, and always wanted to know how he could help her further. She felt free to pick his brains and learn from his experience. The main advice that he gave her, using Sarai's words, was *'to press into the Lord, take refuge in him, trust that he will be working in and through you'*. Sarai realised that this is what Donald had done throughout his life:

> *That is what has got him through a lot in his life. I know from conversations with him that his success, who and how he is now, and how he treats people now, is all testament to how he always brings things back to the Lord.*

Sarai knows how blessed she has been to work for Donald. Even after she left the programme and started full-time work for her MP, Robin Millar, Donald would continue to ask how she was getting on. When Donald turned eighty in April 2024, she and one or two other graduates organised a birthday celebration for him, just to show their appreciation for all that he had done for them and for the care that he continued to show them.

CHAPTER EIGHTEEN

Christians in Parliament

Is This What We Have Really Signed Up For?

We saw in chapter fifteen that despite all of Donald's previous experience of working with different bodies, entering the Lords was something on a much higher plane altogether. As well as getting used to the sheer geography of such a large, ancient building, he had to get himself acquainted with the Lords' rules, protocols and procedures, some arising from the mists of time. There was so much to learn and absorb.

The same problems would be faced by the huge cohort of new Members of Parliament in June 2024, when Labour, under Sir Keir Starmer, won a landslide victory. Entering the Commons were three hundred and fifty new MPs, of whom three hundred and thirty-five were completely new, and fifteen who had been MPs before but not in the 2019–2024 Parliament.[134] This was an enormous number

---

134. Richard Cracknell, 'What do we know about the 2024 cohort of MPs?' (*The House*, 5th November 2024).

of new members, who would all have to learn the ropes associated with their new calling. Isabel Hardman undertook research into the often fraught experiences that new MPs went through as they began their parliamentary careers. She wrote:

> *In interviews with new MPs, I was struck by the strange tension between their shock at the long hours they were working and the creeping realisation that it was possible to be very busy without achieving very much at all.*[135]

MPs enter Parliament with a desire to serve their constituents and their country as best they can, but they face many frustrations as they do so. Is it easier for Christians? Not only do Christians wish to serve their constituency and their country, they also know that they are there to serve their heavenly King. It is of course true that the Holy Spirit will empower Christians to live for Jesus as they carry out their political roles, but he often uses other Christians to give them necessary support. Unfortunately, members who are away from home for much of the week will miss the support of family and their church small group. Donald, for example, admits that he is rarely able to attend his church home group that meets on a Wednesday because he is so often down in London.

This is where the organisation Christians in Parliament is so vital in providing spiritual support and friendship among like-minded people, whatever their party hue is.

---

135.   Isabel Hardman, *Why We Get the Wrong Politicians* (Atlantic Press, 2019), p. 56.

The Organisation Behind Christians in Parliament

Christians in Parliament is an All-Party Parliamentary Group (APPG) that, as its website states, *'exists to support all Members and staff in their work in the Houses of Parliament.*[136] The group provides support to Christians, as its name suggests, but they also offer support to others in Parliament who would not consider themselves to be Christian believers.

Tim Farron, the Liberal Democrat MP for Westmorland & Lonsdale, is the current Chair of the APPG. Donald, along with Marsha de Cordova, Labour MP for Battersea, and Rebecca Smith, Conservative MP for South West Devon, are all officers of the group.

The group is serviced by Rev. Mark Harris, an ordained Church of England minister with previous experience in the financial services sector, and Claire Newman, who was previously Director of Internal Communications for Save the Children International. Mark points out that he and Claire *'serve the All-Party Parliamentary Group and are accountable to Tim, Don and the other officers'.*

Whereas other APPGs are often campaigning groups trying to put pressure on government to amend their policies, Tim Farron sees Christians in Parliament as principally being a fellowship group, *'supporting people who are Christians, and, like any other church, putting the word out there, trying to build relationships and bringing people to faith'.*

---

136. https://www.christiansinparliament.org.uk/about/who-we-are/ (accessed 8/4/25).

Mark sees the ministry as having three components: outreach, discipleship and public theology. Outreach is clearly presenting the Christian faith to those who want to find out more. This is done through personal conversations and inviting parliamentarians to services and more evangelistic events with, for example, interviews with prominent Christians, such as the television presenter Dan Walker. Discipleship is looking to equip Christians to live out their faith in all aspects of their lives, particularly through Bible studies and chapel services. Public theology hopes to give 'a deep Christian anthropology about what it means to be a human being and how that should ground our approach to politics and policy'. This often comes through special events, involving briefings and lectures on particular topics.

In one sense, the work is becoming evermore challenging through the increasing secularisation of society, and Parliament is not immune from that. One way this has been noticed by Tim is that a lot of MPs no longer stand up for prayers at the beginning of the Commons' day. They are in the chamber to reserve their seats for the rest of the day, a bit like, as he put it, 'the parliamentary equivalent of holidaymakers of a certain nationality putting their towels on their sun loungers to reserve them for the day'. Donald knows that they lost 'very good friends after the 2024 election', and they have had to go out and look for new members to join Christians in Parliament. Rebecca Smith, one of the officers, is one such new member.

Vital Fellowship

The key meeting that brings Christian parliamentarians together is the Wednesday morning Bible study. Either Mark or Claire leads the session, which involves the study of a book of the Bible and a time of prayer.

Donald greatly values the weekly Wednesday morning Bible studies as a time of blessing when he can meet with fellow Christians for prayer and Bible study. It puts his role in Parliament in perspective, showing that he is there for a greater purpose, knowing that God is with him in his desire to serve Jesus in the Lords. Rachael Maskell, MP for York Central, expresses the value of these sessions particularly strongly by claiming that '*they are the most precious time in the week*'. She appreciates the fact that the group consists of all ages, from different denominations and with different party allegiances, but also that '*party politics stops at the door*'. She has created deep relationships with members of the group that have lasted for years. A quiet word in the corridor has been '*a huge encouragement*', as she has tried to grapple with difficult political issues.

She sees Donald as '*an inspiring colleague and friend in Westminster, someone who always brings nuggets of real wisdom to share, treasure that you want to store up and reflect on*'. She gains particular blessing from the agricultural illustrations that he uses in the studies.

Rachael summarises the value of the group as it enables members '*as we rise above politics and tribe to make sense of the strange place we are called to, to walk in unity in encouraging one another as we read scripture and pray weekly together'.* The group helps Rachael *'to focus on what God has given her to do each day, all for his glory'.*

Tim Farron agrees with Donald and Rachael about the value of the Wednesday morning studies and prayer time, especially as he finds it very difficult to have midweek contact with his own church, partly because he is in London and partly because he is, as he put it, *'stupidly busy'.*

Those who meet are from different parties, but party differences are put to one side. Tim describes his group as consisting of *'pro-Brexit Conservatives, going all the way through to Corbyn-supporting Labour people, but all with the same theology'.* As Donald explains:

> *Any confrontational activity that normally takes place in the House is absolutely put to one side, as people meet around the scriptures and to talk about the Lord, united in Christ.*

Mark adds:

> *It's not that politics are off the table, but it's just a recognition that we are all united in Christ. It's really important how your faith affects your politics, and to be constantly questioning the grounding for our political convictions. The fact that you are disagreeing on a political issue with a brother or sister in Christ should make you think why you really take this view and ask whether you have truly thought it through. It is a deep, personal fellowship, but at the same time, we do not want to brush political issues under the carpet.*

Tim could only recall one occasion where there was a bit of tension in the room during a Bible study, and that was over the issue of universal credit. He also recalled debating in the chamber on a topic that he felt passionate about when he saw on the opposing benches members of the Bible study group who took a different view. Their presence was a great way of reminding him to '*play the ball and not the man*', and that you can feel passionate about something but still operate in the '*realm of grace*'. For Tim the influence of the group has a permeating effect on how he conducts himself in the Commons and beyond.

There are other events that take place to build up Christians in Parliament. Each Tuesday a short weekly lunchtime service is held in the Chapel of St Mary Undercroft, which is beneath Westminster Hall. This gives Christians the opportunity to worship God and be built up in their lives in Parliament, as well as enabling others with questions to come along and think about issues. In addition, on Thursdays there is a lunchtime prayer meeting for staff to pray for the work of Parliament.

Mark and Claire also provide pastoral support to those who request it, and over the years they have supported some members quite intensively, an important task in the often febrile environment in which members operate. Claire explained it like this:

> *We have a privileged position in the sense that we are non-party political, and so some people feel that they can take down their masks and reveal that they are struggling and finding things a bit harder. They believe*

that they can trust you and because you are on the inside, you will understand.

Special Events

As well as regular weekly meetings, Christians in Parliament organise events, often in response to issues that Parliament is debating. As we mentioned in chapter sixteen, at the time of writing, one of the key Bills that has passed through the House of Commons is the Terminally Ill Adults (End of Life) Bill, a Private Member's Bill sponsored by Labour MP, Kim Leadbetter. This Bill is proposing legislation that promotes assisted suicide. Christians in Parliament is not a campaigning body, but it wants parliamentarians to be aware of the issues associated with what is being proposed in the Leadbetter Bill.

For issues such as assisted suicide, special resources are created and events are held for parliamentary members to think through how to approach such issues. In the case of assisted suicide, briefing notes were produced and sessions were held, as Mark explained, '*to help members recognise that everyone approaches political issues with an underlying worldview of what human life is for, as well as to outline how an underlying Christian view of human life will inform an approach to assisted suicide at an applied policy level*'. Early morning talks in October and November 2024 were addressed by Robert Song, Professor of Theological Ethics at the University of Durham, on the subject of Assisted Dying. These sessions were well attended, including by Kim Leadbetter herself, the Bill's sponsor, and they demonstrated that people had different reasons for opposing assisted suicide.

There have been other lectures on a range of topics such as 'What difference does Christian faith make to the Economy?', 'How should a Christian think about politics?' and 'What difference does Christian faith make to Defence policy?' These lectures have been given by eminent speakers in their fields and are intended to make listeners consider underlying principles that relate to Christian faith and different areas of policy.

Perhaps the most prominent 'special event' is the National Parliamentary Prayer Breakfast, held each year[137] in Westminster Hall.

The 2023 National Parliamentary Prayer Breakfast

Donald was Chair of the 2023 breakfast, when seven hundred people were packed into Westminster Hall for a sumptuous breakfast, wonderful fellowship, beautiful singing, powerful prayers and deep, relevant gospel teaching. Of the seven hundred, two hundred were parliamentarians from both Houses, and most of the rest were church leaders who had invited their MP or had been invited by them. A tremendous gathering with Prime Minister Rishi Sunak also in attendance! To add to the occasion, the beautifully ornate Speaker's State Coach was on display in the corner of the hall. Because of Donald's

---

137. There was no national prayer breakfast in 2024 because of the General Election that took place in June that year.

involvement in organising it, we shall look at this event in more detail to try to capture the flavour of it.

The formal part of the breakfast began with welcomes from Sir Lindsay Hoyle, Speaker of the House of Commons, who asked that the gathering would pray for peace, particularly in Ukraine, and Lord McFall, the Lord Speaker, who emphasised the importance of this event in demonstrating faith and our Christian heritage in our culture and politics. Donald as Chair added his welcome to the gathering, and expressed his gratitude to the many people and parliamentary departments involved in the organisation of the event. He made particular mention of the church leaders in attendance, thanking them for their support by saying, 'We in Parliament need your daily prayers.' He explained that the theme of the breakfast was 'The Power of Forgiveness in Public Life.'

It almost seemed as if the singing during the morning was so rousing that it would lift the ancient rafters of Westminster Hall. It was led with boundless energy by Geraldine Latty-Luce, who describes herself on her website as 'encourager, songwriter, performer, worship leader, vocal coach and choir director'.[138] She was accompanied by her husband Carey and his band, and a choir comprising parliamentary staff and London School of Theology students. Those present in the hall joined in the singing and particularly applauded Gerry and Carey's arrangement of 'Amazing Grace'. It was indeed very moving worship.

---

138. https://geraldinelatty.com/about (accessed 31.03.25).

This occasion was of course first and foremost a prayer breakfast, and so prayers were led by three peers, Lord Stunnell, Baroness Morgan and Lord Weir, along with Carol Monaghan MP. They gave thanks that we live in a parliamentary democracy, that parliamentarians are able to serve people in need, and that we enjoy freedom of worship. Prayers were offered for parliamentarians that they might have wisdom and integrity. Concern was raised in prayer for those in our country and beyond who were facing all sorts of pressures, whether they be financial, family, or health pressures, or the pressures suffered as a result of physical persecution for their faith. Global problems, such as the war in Ukraine, earthquakes in Syria and Turkey, and hunger in Africa, were lifted to God in prayer. Because society seemed to becoming more divisive, prayers were offered that discourse would be carried out in a respectful manner, recognising that we are all made in the image of God. Following the breakfast's theme of forgiveness, prayers were offered that we would all find the forgiveness of the Lord Jesus.

The guest speaker at the breakfast was Amy Orr-Ewing, a well-known theologian and speaker. She also advocates for those who are survivors of abuse and mistreatment. Amy began by sharing how the words sung in Mary's Magnificat at an Evensong service really *'chilled her to the bones'* after spending the day in a criminal court supporting an abuse victim.[139] She went on to talk about the hurt and pain that are experienced by so many in our society and that there is a crying out for justice. She emphasised that forgiveness

---

139. *'He has cast down the mighty from their thrones, and has lifted up the lowly'* (from Luke 1:52).

and civil justice are not mutually exclusive, but we seem in modern Britain to have lost the art of forgiveness. There seems to be more hatred and intolerance shown to those with whom we disagree, including even campaigns of harassment against those with an opposing view. The cruelty that can be shown is similar to that suffered by her own grandparents who had to flee East Germany so as not to be deported to Siberia, and arrived in England with only the clothes on their backs.

Amy proclaimed powerfully how justice and forgiveness are brought together through the person of Jesus Christ, the Son of God, the Incarnate One.

> *The death of the Son of God in history points to the vast value placed on you, including your suffering, by a loving God. Christian forgiveness underlines the seriousness of the hurt and the evil that has occurred, since forgiving it requires the suffering and death of the Son of God. That is not cheap . . . It challenges us to think that we are all flawed in some way or other, and that we all need forgiveness.*

Amy went on to explain how having received forgiveness from God, we can then share that forgiveness with others. She gave a very powerful example of a friend of hers, Benjamin Kwashi, the Archbishop of Jos in northern Nigeria. Benjamin and his family lived in a very dangerous part of the country, where Christians were periodically attacked by terrorist groups. He had three assassination attempts on his life, his wife Gloria suffered a brutal attack, and their house was burned down. They were driven to their knees in prayer. God gave them both the strength to forgive and to carry on serving the people in that community, including terrorist members of the community. They adopted eighty-five orphans, a sign of their generous love for others.

> *They live in a place of incredible tension, with the most outstanding joy and peace that I have ever seen. They live in a flow of forgiveness that builds schools and trains leaders to love across difference. They build churches that serve communities and leads to friendships across divides.*

She invited all to receive forgiveness and with it the power to forgive others. She finished by saying:

> *I believe the power to forgive and to receive forgiveness may just be the greatest gift that the Christian story can offer our age.*

At that point, Geraldine and the choir most appropriately gave their extraordinary rendition of 'Amazing Grace'. Then after Father Alexander Master gave the final blessing, Donald wrapped up the session by giving his final thanks, including to Amy for '*such a challenging and inspiring address*', and inviting participants to join the seminars that would take place after the breakfast.[140]

Identity in Christ

At the end of the livestream broadcast of the 2023 breakfast, Sir Gary Streeter (a Conservative MP at the

---

140. To obtain the full flavour of this prayer breakfast, it can be viewed at https://www.youtube.com/watch?v=PUqHqSUs9GM (accessed 1/4/25).

time) interviewed Rachael Maskell (a Labour MP) and Tim Farron (a Liberal Democrat MP) on what they thought of the breakfast. Both said that they had thoroughly enjoyed Amy's talk, and had got so much from her message that we receive forgiveness from Christ because of his work on the cross, that forgiveness is costly, and that we need to share it with others. Sir Gary summed it up by saying:

> *Here we have a Labour Member of Parliament, here we have a Liberal Democrat Member of Parliament, and a Conservative Member of Parliament, and we are all talking about forgiveness and reconciliation and redemption.*

That is what Christians in Parliament encourages their members to do: to put one's identity in Christ first before one's identity as a politician. People might sit on opposite benches in the House, but if they are together in Christ there is a unity there that transcends party politics. The organisation asks members to think through how their identity in Christ influences their views on particular issues. And if politically the worst comes, and MPs lose their seats in an election or peers lose their positions in the Lords because of constitutional reorganisation, those whose identity lies in Christ will keep that for eternity. Nobody can take that away.

Conclusion

Y Divent Look Like a Sur!

One of Donald's passions is his garden. (In fact, we have already seen in chapter ten that Donald felt that the Lord was warning him not to make an idol out of his garden.) There was one occasion when he wanted to add a boat as a feature to his garden, and so he and Rhoda went to Amble, a fishing port on the Northumberland coast, to see if there was an old boat that they could buy. There they met a fisherman who showed them a boat that seemed just what they were looking for. He said that he would contact the owner for Donald to see if he wanted to sell it and for what price. Donald gave him his card with his name 'Sir Donald Curry' (this was before Donald became a member of the Lords) and phone number so that the owner could contact him. The fisherman looked at the card and he looked at Donald, and, not quite believing what he saw, he looked at the card and Donald again. Then in his strong Amble dialect he exclaimed, '*Ar ee a sur*?' Donald said that he was.

The chap replied, '*If y divent mind me saying so, y divent look like a sur!*'

Of course, we do not know exactly what a '*sur*' is meant to look like, but the point is that Donald comes across as an ordinary man, neither a '*sur*' nor a '*toff*', without any airs and graces. Rather, he has endearing qualities that make him loved and admired by those he works with or comes into contact with.

Sarai Challis, his graduate mentee in 2022–2023 described his warmth thus:

> *When people ask me who I work for, and I say, 'Lord Curry', so often they smile and say, 'He's such a lovely man.' It's true, because he is exceptionally warm. I don't know if that's because he is a Northerner or a believer, or a combination of both. One thing that I have noticed is, which is quite unique for a politician, he is the exact same with everyone he is interacting with, whether that be a peer, a member of staff or the person making his coffee. He has the exact same sense of humour and the exact same ability to put people at ease.*

Others have spoken about his warmth and willingness to make time for people. Dame Fiona Reynolds, a member of the Policy Commission, although admitting that he was an '*unknown quantity*' when she first started to work with him, soon realised that he was '*a lovely, lovely man whose heart is one hundred per cent in the right place*'. Another member of the Commission, Dame Deirdre Hutton, saw him as an excellent Chair who was '*very amiable, jolly, able to chivvy people along, very engaging, able to create a team spirit and made people* want *to work hard*'. Elizabeth Buchanan, who acted as a liaison between Prince Charles and Donald, said of Donald, '*I never heard him say anything nasty about anyone.*' Professor Stuart Reid said, '*I don't know anyone who doesn't warm to him.*'

Linda Radnor worked closely with him at Cawood Scientific, and said about him:

> *He was one of these wonderfully calm people. I never saw him lose his temper or raise his voice, but he could command that table. When we had meetings at the sites, he would go around and chat to the people sweeping the floor, doing the accounts, whatever they were doing, and he was charming. He was interested in everybody, regardless of their age, ethnicity, background or interests, and he would chat to them, making them feel that this was a lovely man.*

Philippa Taylor, who manages the CARE Leadership Programme, spoke very fondly of him:

> *Every time his name is mentioned, people just smile and say that he is an amazing guy. I do feel a great warmth towards him, and I feel very privileged over these past few years to get to know him a bit. He is such an amazing Christian man. He reminds me of my father, grandfather and uncles who were very godly men. He is part of that generation of godly, praying, Christian leaders.*

Gwyn Howells, who worked closely with him on the Meat and Livestock Commission, also felt a personal warmth towards him, from both the professional support that he received but also from the personal support he received at key times such as when his wife died in 1995. Gwyn said:

Don is a people person, and I think that is because of his Christian beliefs. He is very strong on that, and very strong on that throughout the organisation. He always had time for people, and he always talked to people; he was never too busy.

On walking round the Lords with him, the author had the sense that Donald knew everyone in the bustling corridors, and likewise that everyone knew him, and not just those who were powerful Lords and Ladies, but those in relatively low positions. He, for example, asked one of the doormen if he had fully recovered from his operation, not just out of politeness but out of a genuine concern for his health.

Donald cares deeply for other people. This comes from his relationship with Jesus, who himself had a deep, incomparable love for ordinary people that ultimately led to his sacrificial death upon the cross. Although Donald would never claim to have that same sacrificial love that Jesus had, the love of Jesus enables him to care deeply for others.

And because he is by nature a practical man, he tries to show that love by getting alongside others and helping them in practical ways.

Demonstrating Practical Support for Others

Gordon Gatward, one of his closest friends, has been involved with him in various projects, such as the Farming

Help Partnership and Care Farming (previously mentioned in chapters twelve and thirteen). He has spoken of the outstanding spiritual and practical support that Donald has given to him and others. He gave one example of praying with a small number of other Christians involved in agriculture, when he had a strong leading that he should contact Donald to see if he could help to bring others together to pray for the farming industry. He was encouraged by those he was praying with to contact Donald straightaway. Donald, as it happened, had been thinking the same way, and so a prayer group was set up at the Farmers' Club. Gordon described the prayer group as *a tremendous place for sharing, to be open, to be able to seek prayerful advice, and to ask for others' prayers, and Don was an integral part of that*. For Gordon personally, *it was a lifeline*.

In 2023 Gordon contacted Donald about a particularly tragic case of a farmer who had been accused in an inspection report of being *negligent* and *failing to take the standard of care to be expected of a competent farmer*, and, as a result, took his own life. This farmer was well respected and maintained high standards, including being a meticulous record keeper. He had, however, not realised that he had the wrong tags on a small number (only eighteen) of his sheep. He tried to rectify his error in the inspector's presence by phoning up for the correct tags, but the inspection judgement remained. Because of the shame of letting himself and his wife down, and the fear of possibly going to prison over this, tragically the farmer hanged himself.

Donald and Gordon met with the farmer's widow, along with John Stanley, the Chair of the Royal Agricultural Benevolent Institution, so that they were all quite clear about the details leading up to this needless loss of life. Donald then contacted one of the DEFRA ministers, Mark Spencer, whom he knew quite well. Mark met with the widow and, as a result, the Rural Payments Agency amended the training programmes for farm inspectors to ensure they are more sensitive in the way that they address non-compliance. They also changed their terminology, as it was the terminology of negligence and incompetence that particularly upset the farmer. This was a case of Donald spending time with someone who felt aggrieved and let down by a heartless, bureaucratic system, and using his network of contacts to make improvements for the future so that others would not be let down in a similar fashion.

Donald was very generous in his advice to others, and he was looked on by many as their unofficial mentor. We mentioned in chapter four that Donald showed great independence of mind when he chaired NFU Mutual by appointing Lindsay Sinclair, who previously worked for Dutch bank IMG, as Chief Executive, thus breaking the tradition of only appointing homegrown chief executives. Lindsay appreciated the support that Donald gave him and wrote in the book of tributes that the board presented to Donald on his retirement:

I have been helped enormously by your advice and support. It has been a great pleasure for me to have had such a special partnership with you. I consider myself very fortunate indeed to have worked through what the Chinese would call 'interesting times' with such a top-class Chairman.

Tim Mordan had previously worked with Donald in the establishment of the Institute of Agriculture and Horticulture, as we mentioned in chapter nine. He had enjoyed that experience and learned so much from Donald. Tim was now retired as Director of DEFRA, but he still called upon Donald for his '*wise counsel*' as he took on other ventures, and he continued to find him '*incredibly helpful and supportive*'.

James, the Earl of Lindsay, has known Donald for over thirty years. For example, he had been Parliamentary Under Secretary of State for Scotland, with particular responsibility for agriculture, fisheries and the environment, and so his path crossed with Donald many times when he was Chair of the MLC. They sat together on the board of the Scottish Agricultural College, and many other committees. He continues to seek his advice as they meet together in the Lords. He says this about Donald:

He has been my guide and mentor over thirty years. There have been a series of chapters in my life when he has been a constant presence. He has always provided calm, consistent advice, and has always had my back. When I am chairing meetings, I always have in the back of my mind, 'How would Don do it?'

Of course, in his charity work that we described in Part Three, we can see that he has a real desire to change the lives of people for the better. His motivation for setting up At Home was not simply to provide accommodation for his daughter Jane, although that was the starting point. It was to help many vulnerable young people to live in a supported Christian environment, where they can be looked after and be helped to develop their personal and employment skills. As Vice-President of Shaftesbury, the organisation that is continuing the work of At Home, Donald continues to use the expertise that he has developed from those early years.

With his involvement in rural charities, including the Prince's Countryside Fund (now the Royal Countryside Fund), the Farming Help Partnership and Care Farming, one can sense that he wants to provide support to the countryside and its communities that he loves so much. He has been able to use his immense agricultural knowledge, his managerial skills and business sense, along with his vast network of contacts, to try to improve the lives of those living and working in rural communities. Through the various Care Farming initiatives, he has seen vulnerable members of society supported that they might benefit from what the countryside has to offer.

Exactly the same applies to his work with Anglican International Development. He has a passion for the people of South Sudan and longs to see their lives improve 'for now and eternity'. Simon Tustin, the Executive Officer of AID, has said:

> He brings decades of experience as a Christian businessman with an almost unparalleled knowledge of agriculture, and he brings his particular hard-nosed business acumen to the issues faced by the charity.

Donald has a love for God and a love for suffering people, but he wants to ensure that correct procedures are followed, especially in a country like South Sudan where corruption is rife, so that the donations of godly supporters are well used.

God-Given Skills

God has blessed Donald in many ways and has given him skills that he has been able to use in the many different areas of service that he has been involved in. He is a very practical man, and he has been able to use practical skills on the farm from the early days working for his father at Low Burradon, through to the farms that he himself ran with Rhoda as a Northumberland tenant farmer. Although he was not seen as an academic at school, he nonetheless developed the intellectual skills necessary in running successful businesses, chairing high-powered committees, and understanding complex issues in order to make speeches in the Lords. These are very significant skills.

He loves to read and has, for example, a deep knowledge of the Bible; with his tremendous memory he can easily quote biblical verses. In his working life, he has been able to absorb what he has read from a variety of sources and then recall it in different situations. This means that he was always well prepared for board meetings or taking part in debates in the Lords. He also has a wonderful memory of people from the past, and he can remember conversations that he has had with them, almost word for word.

He is a man of initiative. As we saw in chapter three, as a young man frustrated by the process of bagging grain on to trailers on his father's farm, he devised a more efficient method of doing it that required much less effort and got the work done more quickly. Likewise, in the same chapter we saw that he was frustrated by the poor marketing of livestock, and so led the initiative to improve marketing by forming a co-operative, North Country Primestock. He has consistently wanted to make things better. In all the organisations that he served, he would ask the questions, *'Why are we doing it this way? What about trying this instead?'*

He has also enabled others to think differently on the various bodies that he has served. For example, the members of the Policy Commission were strong-minded individuals who possessed a diverse range of views on the future of agriculture. He was highly successful in getting them to recast their thinking so that they came to a final position that they could all sign up to. As Chair of the Better Regulation Executive, he worked to change the culture of government departments so that they would want to reduce the number of regulations imposed on businesses. He also worked to change the culture of regulatory bodies so that they would provide support to businesses that found it difficult to comply with particular regulations, rather than simply beating them with sanctions.

As we have seen throughout the book, Donald has a well-developed skill in chairing meetings. He is able to keep discussion moving in what he believes to be the right direction to reach what he believes to be the best outcome. This means that he has to get people to compromise, with the result that not everyone gets exactly what they want, but the most acceptable solution is reached. In chapter nine we described the working of the Set-Aside Group that was formed to produce an acceptable framework for British farming after the European Union abolished set-aside, a process that paid farmers for taking cropland out of production. There were two completely opposing camps involved in discussions: farmers who wanted to be able to produce more crops and take advantage of rising prices, and environmentalists who did not want to see more land under intensive cultivation. After long months of very tough negotiations, Donald managed to get them to come round to the point of accepting a voluntary set-aside solution.

As someone who never seems to get stressed, Donald is excellent at defusing situations, finding common ground and ultimately acceptable solutions. Meurig Raymond, former President of the National Farmers' Union, had seen him deal with an angry group of Welsh farmers who were complaining about Meat and Livestock Commission levy payments, and being able to calm them down completely. He described Donald as being *'top of the league for diplomacy'*.

Professor Stuart Reid, Principal of the Royal Veterinary College, was full of praise for the way in which Donald chaired meetings *'with military precision'*, as we noted in chapter nine. It was not, however, just the way that he chaired meetings that Stuart admired, but also how he was able to *'convene meetings'*. Stuart explained it thus:

> *He has an amazing ability to convene, and I don't mean chair, but bring together. He is a fantastic guy at bringing people together, almost effortlessly, because people warm to him.*

One example of this is the Agri-Food Charities Partnership, of which Donald is the Patron and Stuart is the Chair. When Donald was Chair of NFU Mutual, he was approached by two trustees of the Perry Foundation, a trust that provided grants for postgraduate agricultural students. They felt that their trust and other small ones like theirs were struggling because of lack of support, as they almost seemed invisible. Donald suggested that they sought support from the NFU Charitable Trust to bring these small trusts together in partnership. This they did, and with Donald's help the Agri-Food Charities Partnership was established, forming a partnership of over a hundred charities. This shows Donald's gift in bringing people together, in line with his philosophy that charitable organisations can achieve so much more in partnership than they can on their own.

What Motivates Donald?

As we look back over Donald's life we see a man who has worked hard on his farm, sat on countless committees and boards, often chairing them, being a peer of the realm, and accumulating some of the highest honours of the land. Most people in their sixties (Donald is now in his eighties!) try to cut down their workload, but for Donald it increased. Professor Stuart Reid quipped, '*He probably doesn't know how to spell "retirement"*'.

So, what has made him take on all these different responsibilities? Is it for self-aggrandisement, or the accumulation of power, or to be looked up to by others who see him as a great man who keeps the company of royalty? Why does he often take on a poisoned chalice, as former

NFU President, Sir Peter Kendall, called his acceptance of the Chair of the Set-Aside Group?

Donald denies that he has taken on these responsibilities to promote himself, but he does admit, *'I cannot deny the excitement of being involved at a high level.'* He has enjoyed working with senior politicians, including prime ministers, senior civil servants and, of course, the King himself. Some of the posts have come out of the blue, such as chairing the Policy Commission, whereas for others he has had to put in a formal application. In all cases, however, it was to serve so that he could have a positive impact to make things better for people.

Furthermore, before accepting the offer of a particular post, or applying for one, he and Rhoda would pray about it to see if it was God's will for them or not. For example, when Donald applied to become a member of the House of Lords, they prayed that God would show them his will. They heard nothing for months, so they assumed that it was not God's will for Donald to enter the Lords. Then Donald received a letter inviting him for interview, and that set him on the road into the Lords.

Whenever Donald takes on a new responsibility he puts tremendous energy into ensuring that he does a good job. James, Earl of Lindsay, says this about Donald's energy and direction:

> *When asked to do something, and he feels that it is right, he will do it. There is no neutral gear with Donald. He wants to see change, and he will never be deflected from what he wants done.*

What motivates Donald? He knows that he has received so much blessing from his life on the land, and so he wants to give some of himself back to the farming industry and rural communities. This is particularly true with regard to his Northumbrian roots. Although so much of his work has been based in London or other parts of the country, he is nonetheless very grateful for the start that he had in Northumberland where he and Rhoda raised their family, and for the pleasure he obtained from his Northumberland farms.

At this stage in his life, he wants to give more support to Northumbria. We have already seen in chapter nine that in 2018 he was involved in establishing the Rural Design Centre to support northern rural communities in new enterprises. He is also President of Community Action Northumberland, which works with village communities to make best use of village halls by refurbishing them, making them available to be used as warm hubs in winter and providing social facilities for local residents. He has also been asked to chair a body run by Northumberland County Council called the Health Equalities Partnership, which aims to provide a multi-agency approach to dealing with some of the significant health problems that exist in different parts of the county.

Donald so much wants to give back to his northern roots. Perhaps, however, a more appropriate question to ask is 'Who motivates Donald? rather than 'What?' We shall consider that fundamental question in our final section.

Micah 6:8

That verse answers the question as to who motivates Donald:

He has shown you, O mortal, what is good. And what does the LORD require of you? To act justly and to love mercy and to walk humbly with your God.

That is probably Donald's favourite verse from the Bible. The Israelite nation in that chapter was being reminded of the grace that God had shown them over the centuries. In return, God was not looking for the performance of religious rituals and sacrifices. Rather he wanted to see in the land, justice and mercy and his people walking humbly with him, acknowledging him as God.

Donald sees that verse as being fundamental as he tries to serve God in humility in different aspects of his life, including his role in the governance of the country in the House of Lords. He is now constantly reminded of these words as his son Jonathan and his daughter-in-law Kate gave him that verse carved on a lovely piece of wood as a Christmas present in 2024. He needs that reminder as he has said:

It is so easy to be seduced by power and influence. It is like an aphrodisiac and very addictive. To walk humbly with God is one of the biggest challenges for those in positions of influence and I am very conscious of that.

Although people see him as a very humble man, he knows that he very often falls short of the standards that God has set. Not long after he started working in the Better Regulation Executive, Francis Maude, a Cabinet Office

Minister, asked him if he was a *'zealot'*, because he would need to be to make the progress expected of him. Donald, as we have commented before, did tackle the job with great zeal, and made considerable changes in the culture of government departments and regulatory bodies.

But did he consider himself a *'zealot'*? As a Christian, he knows that whatever others might think of him, he does not fully live up to the standards of God's calling. He looks to the apostle Paul and admires the zeal that he displayed in spreading the gospel of God's love and forgiveness in the ancient world, planting new churches, and, through all this, demonstrating a deep relationship with Jesus, his Lord and Saviour. *He* was a real zealot – even in the way that he persecuted the church before he became a Christian.

Donald knows that he is not in the same league as Paul. He knows that he does not take every opportunity to share his faith as he should, by challenging others to come to Jesus in repentance and faith. He prays and reads Scriptures daily, but he knows that it is often rushed. He knows that on many occasions he has let his Lord down in what he has said, done and thought and what he has failed to do. He, of course, is not alone in this. All Christians are very much aware of their shortcomings, and that sin, although forgiven by the Lord, still sticks to us and taints us.

Nor should we make the apostle Paul our standard. Paul knew that God's grace was especially poured out on him, and said:

> *The grace of our Lord was poured out on me abundantly, along with the faith and love that are in Christ Jesus. Here is a trustworthy saying that deserves full acceptance:*

Christ Jesus came into the world to save sinners – of whom I am the worst.[141]

Paul knew that Jesus died for him, the worst of sinners, and Donald knows that as well. It is not a question as to how much zeal you have, it is a question as to whether you are looking to Jesus on the cross, know that he has dealt with the awfulness of your sin and whether you are allowing him to control your life as King.

Donald likes the picture that Paul gave of the people of Israel in the desert drinking from the rock that is Christ:

They all ate the same spiritual food and drank the same spiritual drink; for they drank from the spiritual rock that accompanied them, and that rock was Christ.[142]

Donald sees his relationship with Christ as vital, as he obtains power and strength from him, drinking from the rock that is Christ. And, of course, he is not alone in doing this: he is in the huge company of Christ's people. These are the many Christian friends that he has, including those in his home church, those with whom he works and prays in different organisations and, of course, the Christians in Parliament group.

There is one person who is absolutely key in Donald's life, and that is, of course, Rhoda. They have been married for almost sixty years and in that time they have drunk from the rock that is Christ together. Donald is quite clear that he could not have done all that he has done without Rhoda's

141.   1 Timothy 1:14-15
142.   1 Corinthians 10:3-4

love and support. As he has said, they have been through lots of valleys together, but they came through together, through their shared faith in Jesus. They have stuck to the three biblical commands that Ian Ross gave them on their wedding day: '*Consider*', '*Commit*' and '*Continue*'.

Together they have been motivated to serve God and others over all these years – and all to God's glory.

Acknowledgements

In writing this book on Donald Curry's life, I am very grateful for the time that he spent with me sharing his memories and recounting both the main events of his life and some of the many conversations that he has had with people from all walks of life. I am also grateful for all the boxes of papers that he deposited with me to help me in my research. (My wife, Ella, although very supportive of my writing, was less enthusiastic about all the boxes that appeared.) Rhoda also shared with me some of her memories, particularly of their early years together and family life.

Donald also pointed me in the direction of key people who were able to give me their particular insights into Donald's work, character and achievements. These very busy people were only too pleased to give up some of their valuable time to talk to me about Donald (or Don, as most of them called him).

Keith Lee and John Murray gave me their recollections of his ministry as a young Christian man, and the development of 'squashes'.

I had very helpful online conversations with a number of colleagues who had been involved with him in his work with the National Farmers' Union and the Meat and Livestock Commission: Bob Bansback, Elizabeth Buchanan, Gwyn Howells, Tony Pexton, Meurig Raymond and Glen Sanderson. Iain Ferguson, Dame Deirdre Hutton and Dame Fiona Reynolds spoke with enthusiasm about working with Donald on the Policy Commission. I was greatly helped in understanding some of Donald's other work in institutions linked to the land and livestock by Caroline Fowle, Simon Green, Linda Radnor, Professor Stuart Reid and John Varley.

I had the pleasure of finding out more about his charitable work by speaking to Rev. Dr Gordon Gatward, John Purves, Ian Simpson and Simon Tustin.

Donald organised a wonderful day for me at the House of Lords when I had the opportunity to meet some of his colleagues, in particular Lord Ewan Cameron, James, Earl of Lindsay, and Lord Sandy Trees, who each gave me useful guidance on the operation of the House of Lords and their insight into Donald's contribution as a peer. I also had an excellent lunch with some members of the Christians in Parliament group, particularly Tim Farron MP, Rev. Mark Harris and Claire Newman, who each made me more aware of the influence that Christians, including Donald, can have in Parliament. Rachael Maskell MP, a key member of the group, was not able to be present for lunch but I met her on another occasion. I was also fortunate to meet Tim Mordan, former Director of DEFRA, who was visiting Donald that day, and he shared some of the wisdom that he had received from Donald. During the day I was splendidly looked after by Henrietta Edwards, Donald's CARE graduate mentee for 2024–2025.

With regard to Donald's work in the Lords, I am also grateful for the conversations that I had with Simon Calvert, Deputy Director of the Christian Institute, Philippa Taylor, Director of the Institute of Faith and Culture at CARE, and Sarai Challis, Donald's CARE graduate mentee in 2022–2023.

In the same way that Donald relies completely on Rhoda, I know that I rely absolutely on Ella, who has to put up with so much, especially during intensive writing periods. I am forever grateful for her love and support.

This is the third book that I have had published by Malcolm Down and Sarah Grace Publishing. As ever, Malcolm has provided excellent support and advice, and has thus made my role easier.

Jim Cockburn
September 2025